THE BEST OF
WELLINGTON

SB

SARAH BENNETT BOOKS

for Lee, with love and thanks

Published by Sarah Bennett Books
PO Box 24-103, Wellington, New Zealand
www.sarahbennettbooks.co.nz

First edition, November 2003
ISBN 0-473-09381-2

Edited & typeset by Sarah Bennett
Internal design by Rose Miller, Parlour, Wellington
Cover design by Eyework, Wellington
Cartography by Alan Brown Graphics, Wellington
Printed by Astra Print, Wellington
Front cover photograph by Craig Potton
Back cover photographs (L–R): Nick Servian (1–3)
and The Kennett Brothers (4)

Contents

Karori Wildlife
Sanctuary

A portion of proceeds from this
book will be donated to the
Karori Wildlife Sanctuary.

About This Book

This book is brought to you by people who live in Wellington and love it. We asked more than 50 Wellingtonians to tell us what they liked best in their city, and we hope the results of our research ensure you enjoy every moment you spend in New Zealand's stunning capital.

The focus of this book is **Wellington City,** with the highlights of its regional neighbours also included (*Porirua*, *Kapiti*, the *Hutt Valley* and *Wairarapa*).

No payment was received in return for any listing in *The Best of Wellington*.

This book is the first published by Sarah Bennett Books, proudly produced in co-operation with many local people. Together we have endeavoured to provide information that is accurate and error-free, but we're counting on you to help us keep it fresh. **Your support will ensure that** *The Best of Wellington* **thrives and develops every year.**

Feedback is welcome, including corrections and suggestions for the next edition. All correspondence will be acknowledged by the editor.

Please write to:

Sarah Bennett Books
PO Box 24-103, Wellington
email: sbbooks@paradise.net.nz
www.sarahbennettbooks.co.nz

This book has been created with the generous assistance of people from the following organisations.

EYEWORK

ASTRA PRINT

Absolutely POSITIVELY Wellington
Me Heke ki Pōneke
Wellington City Council

Department of Conservation
Te Papa Atawhai

greater WELLINGTON
THE REGIONAL COUNCIL

MagnumMac

ULTRACOPY
CENTRE

CRAIG
POTTON
PUBLISHING

Acknowledgements

The publisher gratefully acknowledges the assistance of the following people who helped make this book: Archetype & Afineline, Aro Valley CAB, Anna Aplin, All Bennetts, Steve Atwell, Bruce Caddy, Robert Chisholm, Phil Dickson, Janet Dunn, Barbara Fill, Mark Fry, Linda Goss, Jane Harris, Jacquie Harper, Holden Hohaia, Geraldine Hulls, Eric Vaughn Holowacz, Susanna Joe, Lindsay Keats, Jonathan Kennett, Carol Knutson, Laura Kroetsch, Malcolm Laird, Tony Lines, LPF Wellington, Brett Mason, Bree Mackay, Danyl McLauchlan, Allan Marshall, Sally-ann Moffat, Mount Pleasant Road, Natacha & Jason, Andy Nelson, Michael Neville, Mike Oates, Chris Orsman, Paddy & Jane, Neal Palmer, Marlene Pope, Amanda Powell, Phil Reed, Dr Michael Revell, Catriona Robertson, Betty Ruffell, Rochelle Selby-Neal, Slater Family, Trecia Smith, Maggie Tait, Nandor Tanczos, Jim & Jan Thomas, Urs & Walt, Wayne Tacon, Penny Wallwork, Tim & Irene Walshe and Lindy Wilson. Thanks to the rest of you too.

Many thanks to contributing writers: Adam Bennett, Lucy Bennett, Dr Hamish Campbell, Chris Dillon, Mike Houlahan, Barbara Mitcalfe, Sarah Pritchett and Lee Slater.

For provision of content and proofreading, a big thank you to the Department of Conservation, Greater Wellington Regional Council and Positively Wellington Tourism.

Invaluable assistance in producing this book came from Rose Miller of Parlour, Nicki McLeod and Fiona Palmer of Alan Brown Graphics, Peter Dorn & Hermann Taufale of Astra Print, Simon Cauchi, David Cauchi, Nick Servian, Katrin, Clem & all at Eyework, and the team at Craig Potton Publishing, especially Betzy Iannuzzi, Ross Blick and Robbie Burton. Special thanks to Bridget Williams whose excellent tutelage helped this book happen.

Thanks also to Kerry McCarty, Mayor Kerry Prendergast, and many other Wellington City Council staff who gave their time and a grant towards the printing of this book.

Sarah Bennett, Editor

Glossary

Aotearoa	New Zealand; *land of the long white cloud*
aroha	*love*
ATM	automatic teller machine; hole in the wall
barista	Italian term for an experienced bar person, now commonly used to denote a skilled coffee maker
BYO	bring your own (bottle of wine to a restaurant)
dairy	corner shop; grocery store
EFTPOS	electronic funds transfer at point of sale (pay at the counter with your ATM card)
gidday	*good day*; hello
kia ora	*be well*; hello; greetings
koha	*gift*; donation
Maui	legendary fisherman who caught the North Island (*te Ika a Maui* – the fish of Maui)
paua	native abalone with a beautiful blue shell
tangata whenua	*people of the land*; local people
Te Papa	*our place*; the National Museum
Te Waipounamu	*the water of greenstone* (jade); the South Island
town belt	a belt of parkland in the city, vested in the local authority and reserved for public use
tramp	hike; trek; bush walk
Whanganui a Tara	*great harbour of Tara*; Maori name for Wellington

Welcome to Wellington

Kia ora, talofa, ni hao, seehtahy, dobro dosli, malo e lelei, nisa bula, yiasou, kia orana, namaste and vanakam!

Welcome to Wellington, Port Nicholson, Wellywood, Middle-earth, *Te Waha o Te Ika* and *Te Whanganui a Tara*. Perched on the edge of a spectacular harbour, encircled by green, towering hills, Wellington is a stunning and compact city with everything you'd expect and much, much more. We Wellingtonians are proud of our city and reckon there's something here for everyone. We delight in showing our visitors around, and that's why we've created this guide: so you can enjoy *The Best of Wellington.*

The city centre is vibrant, exciting and friendly, combining the hustle and bustle of a big city with the quirkiness of a charming village. There's culture galore in our museums and galleries, plenty of quality entertainment, fabulous food, spectacular shops, a wonderful waterfront and fascinating diversions such as beautiful buildings and street art.

A 2003 survey found that Wellingtonians rate their quality of life more positively than any other New Zealand city's residents, with 39% rating it as 'extremely good'.

Exploring Wellington on foot is highly recommended as many attractions are within an easy stroll. Don't be put off by the hills! Take your time and enjoy the fresh air and views. Zigzagged steps and hidden shortcuts abound; parks and reserves make scenic thoroughfares and locals will happily help you find your way.

The great outdoors is on the doorstep for those who want some beach or bush. Along with neighbouring Porirua, Kapiti, the Hutt Valley and Wairarapa, the Wellington region will amaze you with its scenic beauty and diverse opportunities for exploration and enjoyment. From the mountainous peaks of the Tararuas in the north to the rocky southern shore, getting out and about is easy and rewarding.

Such are the wonders of New Zealand and Wellington — the civic centre now turned sophisticated tourist destination. One moment you're living the high life in the downtown nightclub quarter. The next you're roaring over a cliff on a 300cc motorcycle tasting the freshest of air. SUNDAY TELEGRAPH, AUSTRALIA

Fascinating Facts

- Wellington is the world's most southern capital and the only capital in the 'Roaring Forties' latitudes.
- Wellington was the first capital city to see in the new millennium.
- Nearly all Wellington residents live within 3 km of the sea.
- Wellington City's population is 174,600 and the whole region 425,000.
- The population mix is around 77% European, 7% Maori, 5% Pacific Island, 9% Asian and 2% other origin.
- Wellington was named New Zealand's 'Top Town' in 2000 by *North & South* magazine — the coveted award for being the best place to live in New Zealand.
- Wellington's sister cities are Sakai, Japan; Harrogate, England; Xiamen, China; and Hania, Crete, and Wellington is special friends with Sydney, Beijing, Taipei and Tianjin. We like everyone else in the world too.

Back to Nature

The settlers of Wellington have greatly altered what was a magnificent landscape of great beauty and diversity. What would it have looked like before we arrived?

Wellington's indigenous vegetation evolved through climate changes spanning many millennia. The tough, small-leaved trees and shrubs and hardy tussocks of the ice ages alternated with warmer periods during which **kauri** grew here. Few of Wellington's forest giants remain, and you won't see the masses of luxuriant epiphytes that perched high and low on them. Tree trunks and any available niche on the ground were clothed in **mosses** and **liverworts** competing with **ferns** and delicate **orchids** to display their myriad hues and textures.

Early European settlers were astounded at the lush 'tropical' appearance of our bush, a contrast to the open, park-like forests they were expecting in these temperate latitudes. Here, tangles of looping lianes such as **kiekie**, climbing **rata** and **supplejack** twined and clung to the massive trunks of **totara**, **pukatea**, **rimu**, **miro**, **matai** and **kahikatea**. Tall **tree fern** species, ferns-that-are-trees, raised their elegant umbrellas to the canopy or arched their graceful fronds in the dimness of the understorey.

Warmer sites were favoured by the candelabra-branched **tawa**, and by **kohekohe**, with its cauliflorous flowers sprouting profusely straight from the trunk, in mid-winter. Here too, spiky **nikau**, our only palm and the southernmost palm species in the world, with its unmistakeable columnar trunk and sculptural, bulbous frond bases, flourished in the damp gullies among an extraordinary diversity of fern species.

On the higher slopes, thousands of **northern rata** reached to over 30 metres high, flowering at Christmas and turning the hills crimson for weeks on end, to the delight of nectar-seeking **tui** and **korimako**.

In the north and east, on well-drained spurs, **beech forest** spread its comparatively uniform canopy. On the swampy valley floors **kahikatea** towered above, and in the areas of open water were extensive groves of **cabbage trees**, **swamp toetoe** and **flax**.

On the shores of Cook Strait a remarkably rich macro-algae (**seaweed**) flora flourished. Estuaries teemed with aquatic and salt-tolerant plants in broad, subtle colour bands, and dunes were clothed in a pelt of silver **spinifex** and golden **pingao**, with handsome plumes of coastal **toetoe** waving high overhead.

The best places to go to see native forest in Wellington are *Otari–Wilton's Bush* and the native forest remnants in the *Botanic Garden* (see GARDENS, PARKS AND PLAYGROUNDS).

By Barbara Mitcalfe, Member, Wellington Botanical Society Inc.
For more information visit www.wellingtonbotsoc.wellington.net.nz

New Zealand bush scene showing punga, toetoe and rimu, with Maori warrior hiding in the shade. Watercolour drawing (around 1846) by Charles Emilius Gold, 1809–71.

Alexander Turnbull Library, Wellington, New Zealand, A-288-021.

Maori Discovery and Settlement

According to Maori legend, **Maui** is said to have fished up the North Island of New Zealand, *Te Ika o Maui*, from his great canoe (the South Island). Maui and his brothers struggled with the large fish, beating and slashing it so that it writhed in agony creating the hills and the valleys. When the fish died it became a great land where previously there had been nothing but ocean. The southern part of the North Island is said to be the head of the fish, *Te Upoko o te Ika*, Wellington Harbour the mouth of the fish, *Te Waha o te Ika*, and Lake Wairarapa the eye of the fish, *Te Whatu o te Ika*.

The Maori explorer **Kupe** is credited with the discovery of the land and harbour on which Wellington is now situated. Kupe sailed his canoe to New Zealand around 950AD, stopping at various points around the new country including what is now Wellington.

Over the next 950 years a succession of Maori people from different tribes arrived and occupied the area including **Tara** and *Tautoke*, sons of *Whatonga* from the Mahia peninsula. Tara was sent by his father to inspect the lower North Island in the twelfth century. He returned after a year, declaring that the best place he had seen was 'at the very nostrils of the island'. It was Tara whose name was given to the harbour, still in use today – **Te Whanganui a Tara**, meaning the Great Harbour of Tara.

Whatonga, Tara and their people shifted south, and were thus the first *iwi* (tribe) in Wellington, hence named *Ngai Tara*. Ngai Tara eventually amalgamated with another iwi, *Ngati Ira*. Other iwi associated with the area were *Ngati Kahungunu*, *Ngai Tahu* and *Ngati Mamoe*.

At the beginning of the nineteenth century, iwi from Taranaki and Kawhia migrated from their ancient homelands to settle in and around Te Whanganui a Tara. These iwi included *Ngati Toa*, *Ngati Ruanui*, *Taranaki*, *Ngati Tama* and *Te Atiawa*. Their settlements and cultivations ringed the inner harbour, with *kainga* (villages) located at Pipitea, Kaiwharawhara, Pitoone, Ngauranga, Te Aro and elsewhere. There was frequent contact and trade between the various *hapu* (sub-tribes) of different kainga, and the harbour was well used as a highway for communication and to gather marine resources. The surrounding bush and streams were all rich sources of food and other supplies for daily life. Whether it was *tuna* (eels) from the many streams that fed the harbour, *harakeke* (flax) from Motukairangi (Miramar Peninsula), or *totara* for *waka* (canoes) and *whare* (houses), from the dense bush further inland to the west, the iwi were in every sense *kaitiaki* (guardians) of their environment.

European Settlement

Abel Tasman (in 1642) and Captain Cook (in 1773) tried to enter Wellington harbour, but were repelled by high winds, and it wasn't until the *New Zealand Company*, led by Edward Gibbon Wakefield, 'purchased' land in the area that settlement began, around 1840. Wakefield named the town after Arthur Wellesley, the first Duke of Wellington (1769–1852), the famous general and British prime minister from 1828 to 1830. (It was previously referred to by Pakeha as Port Nicholson, named after an Australian harbour master by a benevolent British captain.)

Settlement of Wellington by the New Zealand Company. A gathering of pioneer ships on 8 March 1840, as described by E. G. Wakefield. chromolithograph by Matthew Thomas Clayton, 1831–1922.

Alexander Turnbull Library, Wellington, New Zealand, C-033-005.

The first anniversary of Wellington was first celebrated in 1841, one year after the arrival of the settler ship *Aurora*, which arrived on 22 January 1840 with 150 settlers after a four-month voyage from England. Other early settler ships included the *Tory, Cuba, Oriental, Roxburgh, Adelaide, Glenbervie, Bolton* and *Coromandel* – all remembered in Wellington street names. Settlers were allocated two lots: an acre in the township, and a back country block worth £1 per acre. Some settlers were a little surprised when they discovered their estate, purchased sight unseen, wasn't exactly 'flat section, all day sun'!

In fact, Wellington began as a settlement with very little flat land. As luck would have it though, a large earthquake in 1855 raised more flat land (read about earthquakes on the next page). This initiated the first major reclamation, and by 1900 the original shoreline had all but disappeared and in its place was a bustling port town.

Wellington didn't start out as New Zealand's capital city. In 1863 the Parliament at Auckland decreed that 'it has become necessary that the seat of government ... should be transferred to some suitable locality in Cook Strait'. The reason? There was concern that the gold-rich southerners of New Zealand would form a separate colony, and a group of Australian commissioners gave the 'objective' opinion that Wellington, with its harbour and central location, would suit best. The Parliament at Wellington (population then 4900) sat for the first time 26 July 1865.

Manawhenua and The Treaty of Waitangi

Today the *manawhenua* (Maori local guardianship) interests in Te Whanganui a Tara are administered by the Wellington Tenths Trust/Nga Tekau o Poneke, which comprises descendants from the iwi of Taranaki, Ngati Tama, Ngati Ruanui and Te Atiawa. Ngati Toa also has interests within Wellington City.

In May 2003 the *Waitangi Tribunal* released its report on the Wellington district claim – *Te Whanganui a Tara me ona Takiwa*. This report is essential reading for those interested in learning about the history of the city and breaches of The Treaty of Waitangi which occurred during its establishment. The Tenths and Ngati Toa are today working with the Crown to negotiate a resolution of their historical grievances. This may take some time, but many agree that it is important in Wellington, as it is elsewhere in New Zealand, to acknowledge the wrongs of the past and commit to a future where both Treaty partners can live in harmony.

Geology of Wellington

New Zealand is known as the Shaky Isles for good reason, and Wellington gets its fair share of tremors each year.

Underneath Wellington, the hard 'basement' rocks of Earth's crust are known as *greywacke*, essentially sandstone with a silt or mud content. They are believed to be 215–200 million years old. The sediment accumulated as horizontal layers on the sea floor offshore of the Queensland sector of **Gondwanaland**. Now they are vertical and far removed from their source rocks in Australia.

In Wellington the greywacke is almost 'naked' – there is just a thin veneer of younger sediment covering it. Most of this sediment is *loess*, wind-blown sand and silt from the exposed sea floor during successive glacial periods of the Ice Ages. Loess forms the conspicuous yellow-brown clay around Wellington.

New Zealand straddles a segment of the collision boundary between two of Earth's 15 major crustal plates – the **Australian Plate** and the **Pacific Plate**. The Australian Plate is moving northwards and the Pacific Plate westwards. The resultant collision is responsible for the northeast–southwest orientation of New Zealand. The entire North Island is on continental crust at the very eastern edge of the Australian Plate. Oceanic crust of the Pacific Plate is being sucked into Earth's crust beneath the eastern coast of North Island.

The collision between plates is responsible for almost all topographic features of the New Zealand landscape. In the Wellington region, the collision is compressing Earth's crust in an east–west direction, almost like squeezing a corrugated sheet – the ridges go up and the valleys go down. This explains some of the landforms around Wellington. But at the same time, the crust is being sheared sideways so that when the faults move they do so both vertically and sideways at the same time.

There are several major faults in the Wellington region, all of which are considered active – in other words they have all moved in the last 100,000 years. These faults are all sideways faults with significant vertical movement and they all cut right through the crust, which is about 25 km thick beneath Wellington.

Wellington City is built along the southern edge of Wellington Harbour, an erosional feature that formed between a master fault, the ***Wellington Fault***, and a set of smaller faults at an angle to it. Most of Wellington City is built within 3 km of the Wellington Fault.

The Hutt motorway snakes along the eroded scarp of the Wellington Fault but the actual fault is tens of metres offshore.

Institute of Geological and Nuclear Scienecs Ltd (Lloyd Homer).

The Wellington Fault last moved in about 1450AD. It moves, on average, every 400–700 years, and there are claims there is a 10 percent chance it will move within the next 50 years. It could move up to 1.5 m vertically and 3 m horizontally, the earthquake potentially exceeding 7.5 on the Richter Scale.

Some areas of Wellington City are built on reclaimed land or relatively unconsolidated sediment, but most dwellings are built on solid rock or very stiff sediment. In a major earthquake there will be some shaking, liquefaction, landslides and possible tsunami in the harbour, but most of the city will be relatively unscathed. Wellington has more than 10,000 buildings, of which only 300 are regarded as substandard from an earthquake-engineering point of view. Wellington's buildings are well constructed and designed, and some public buildings are supported by state of the art 'base isolator' foundation bearings. You can see one of these up close at *Te Papa*.

The **Wairarapa Fault**, on the east of the Rimutaka Range on the horizon east of Wellington, last moved in 1855. It was a huge earthquake with devastating consequences. Fortunately only about 3000 people were living in Wellington and only one person was killed. The fault ruptured over more than 156 km and moved a maximum of 6.5m vertically and 13m sideways in places. Happily, this fault is not expected to move for hundreds of years, but when it does the associated earthquake is expected to exceed magnitude 8.

By Dr Hamish Campbell, geologist,
Institute of Geolgical and Nuclear Sciences & Te Papa

For more information about New Zealand's geological activity …

visit www.gns.cri.nz – the home of the Institute of Geological and Nuclear Sciences.

visit www.geonet.org.nz – this sites contains real-time monitoring and data collection for rapid response and resesarch into earthquake, volcano, landslide and tsunami hazards.

see the *Awesome Forces* display at Te Papa, and view the 'quake breakers' underneath the building.

Wellington Weather

Famous for glorious blue sky, warm summers and mild winters, Wellington was New Zealand's sunniest main centre in 1995, 1997 and 2000! However, some would allege that the wind blows well above the national average, so we asked the experts to give us the low-down on Wellington weather.

Q. *We heard that Wellington gets more than 2000 **sunshine hours** per year. How does that compare to New Zealand's average?*

A. The national average is around 1955 hours per year.

Q. *That must make it pretty warm! What's the usual **summer daily temperature** range?*

A. It's usually 13.4–20.3°C (56–69°F).

Q. *What about **winter averages**?*

A. In winter you could expect an average daily temperature range of 6.2–11.3°C (43–52°F), so it's pretty mild. The skies are often bright and very clear.

Q. *I'm sure they are, but it must rain sometimes!*

A. Sure it does. In fact the **annual rainfall** is around 1246 mm – that compares to a national average of 1375mm.

Q. *Is it true about the wind?*

A. What about the wind?

Q. *You know, 'windy Wellington'. It's pretty windy here, right?*

A. Yes, the **average wind speed** (recorded at the Kelburn station) is 21.8 km/hr compared to a national average of 18.1 km/hr, but what you have to remember is that the Cook Strait is a big gap in the mountain ranges that stretch from East Cape to Fiordland, and the wind funnels through this gap.

Q. *Tell me about these **famous southerlies** then.*

A. They're actually not as common as the norwester – that's our prevailing wind direction, and it can get a bit gusty.

Q. *You changed the subject. What's the story with the southerlies?*

A. Well, when it's coming, we know we're in for a 'cold snap', and sometimes they are furious – closing the airport and stopping the ferries. But they can generally be relied on to give way to clear conditions, so they're really not that bad.

Q. *How bad can they get?*

A. Our most famous southerly storm was in 1968, when the ferry *Wahine* was blown on to Barrett Reef. That was our worst storm on record – wind gusts were believed to have reached 240 km/h!

For more information about New Zealand weather, visit:

www.niwa.co.nz
– ***National Institute of Water & Atmospheric Research*** (Taihoro Nukurangi), where the national climate data base is located.

www.metservice.co.nz
– home of the ***MetService***, provider of weather information including forecasts.

Nick Servian

Attractions and Activities

Wellington is city of pleasant surprises. You'll probably already know about our most famous attractions, but just wait until you see what else there is to do ...

Most of these attractions and activities are open every day. On public holidays (see USEFUL INFORMATION) opening hours are usually the same as Sundays, although nearly everything will be closed on Christmas Day. Many have wheelchair access and welcome children. Your hosts are eager to look after you, so do let them know if you have any questions or special requirements. For special events, see the EVENTS CALENDAR or try the following websites:

Feeling Great! (www.feelinggreat.co.nz) A programme of happy, healthy fun brought to you by *Wellington City Council*.

Wellington Visitor Information Centre (www.wellingtonnz.com) Follow the events link for an up-to-date events calendar.

Museums, Galleries and Heritage Tours

TE PAPA

Cable Street, tel 381-7000, www.tepapa.govt.nz

Te Papa, New Zealand's national museum, is housed in an eye-catching building on the waterfront. Priceless ancient treasures stand side by side with state-of-the-art technology to tell the stories of the land and its people. The *Washington Post* described it as 'one of the most ambitiously eclectic museums in the world'.

'Hands-on' exhibitions such as *Awesome Forces* use interactive exhibits to show you the forces that shaped New Zealand's unique landscape. A diverse range of animals and plants and their habitats are displayed in *Mountains to Sea*, while *Bush City* is an outdoor area where plants and rock forms bring the natural environment to life.

The stories and customs of the Maori are celebrated in *Mana Whenua* – an exhibition featuring many beautiful taonga (treasures). A stunning contemporary marae (gathering place) and exhibitions showcasing contemporary Maori art give a unique insight into New Zealand's indigenous people.

Dramatic tales of immigration are told in *Passports*, while *Mana Pasifika* celebrates the diversity of the country's Pacific cultures. Several galleries display the best of New Zealand and international art and culture in an exciting range of short- and long-term exhibitions.

The four *Discovery Centres* offer a variety of creative and interactive activities for children aged 7–12, while those under 5 will love the daily storytelling and dress-up sessions at *StoryPlace*. The *Time Warp* is popular with visitors of all ages. Take a time travel ride, or enjoy 'virtual' bungy jumping, sheep shearing and other classic Kiwi activities.

Te Papa's facilities include *Foodtrain* for fast food and *Espresso*, catering to those needing their fix. There are two gift shops. Extensive parking is available outside and underneath Te Papa at a daily maximum cost of $8.

You should allow at least half a day to explore Te Papa, though it can take much longer! Introductory tours leave from the information desk at 10.15am and 2pm ($9; bookings not required).

Admission free, though charges apply to some short-term exhibitions and the Time Warp. *Open* daily 10am–6pm, and until 9pm on Thursdays.

MUSEUM OF WELLINGTON CITY AND SEA

Bond Store, Queens Wharf, tel 472-8904, www.museumofwellington.co.nz

Wellington's museum tells the capital's stories of both sea and land, and is housed in a significant heritage building, the restored 1892 Bond Store (customs house). The museum's galleries include *A Millennium Ago* where Maori legend combines with special effects, and the *Wahine Gallery*, a memorial to the 1968 maritime tragedy (see page 52). A giant cinema screen takes visitors on a journey through Wellington's past, present and future. *By The Sea We Live* celebrates the city's maritime history, and the *Wellington Gallery* presents the social history of Wellington since Maori settlement. The *Plimmer's Ark Gallery* displays part of the excavated remains of the *Inconstant* (built in 1848), while the bow section remains under the floor of the now restored **Old Bank Shopping Arcade** (see SHOPPING). Tours available. *Admission* free. *Open* daily 10am–5pm.

CITY GALLERY WELLINGTON – TE WHARE TOI

Civic Square, tel 801-3952, www.city-gallery.org.nz

Popular hotspot, the City Gallery Wellington has forged a reputation for challenging and innovative exhibitions of art, architecture and design, presenting significant New Zealand artists alongside major international figures. A landmark building, varied exhibition programme and a wide range of public programmes cater to a broad audience. Free public tours run every Sat/Sun at 1pm; no bookings required. The *Nikau Gallery Café* on site has a courtyard and welcomes children. *Admission* free for local programmes, some admission fees may apply. *Open* daily 10am–5pm.

CABLE CAR MUSEUM
Top of the Cable Car, 1 Upland Road, Kelburn, tel 475-3578,
www.cablecarmuseum.co.nz
At the top of the cable car, Wellington's newest museum tells the
story of one of the city's most visited attractions, the cable car
system, which started service in 1902. The museum is housed in the
old winding house and displays a cable car and trailer, photographs,
film and the machinery that originally operated the system.
The museum has a small shop selling models, books, videos and
souvenirs. *Admission* free. *Open* (1 Nov–Easter) daily 9.30am–5.30pm;
(rest of year) daily 9.30am–5pm. To ride the cable car, see CITY
LOOKOUTS.

Richard Seddon,
then Prime Minister,
and other gentlemen
at the launch of the
cable car service in
1902.
*K.A. Wilson Collection, Alexander
Turnbull Library, Wellington,
New Zealand, F-135995-1/2.*

CARTER OBSERVATORY
Top of the Cable Car, Wellington Botanic Garden, tel 472-8167,
www.carterobs.ac.nz
Explore the wonders of the universe and spend time with the stars.
Look through the telescope, view displays, marvel at the night sky
in the planetarium or take a journey of imagination through the
wonders of space in the current feature show. *Admission* adult $10,
child $5, (show costs vary). *Open* Sun–Tues 10am–5pm; Wed–Sat
10am–late. *Planetarium shows:* Mon–Fri (school term) 11.35am; Sat/
Sun/public & school hols 12.15pm–4.25pm, and evenings on Tues/
Thur/Sat. *Telescope sessions:* Wed–Sat evenings (weather permitting;
dusk onwards). Solar telescope sessions daily 12.30pm–2.45pm.
Telescope session admission (including planetarium show) adult $20,
child $15,(family concessions available). Gold coin entry on last
Sunday of the month.

CAPITAL E

Civic Square, tel 913-3720, www.capitale.org.nz

Directly under the city-to-sea bridge you'll see Capital E, a creative technology and performance centre for children and families. It stages professional theatre, hands-on exhibitions, events and school holiday programmes. Capital E also houses the *SoundHouse*, a video and sound engineering suite, and *ONTV*, a fully equipped television studio for children. Great fun with high technology! The exhibitions and *Play Ground* (a fabulous toy shop) ensure there's always something to see. Fully equipped for people with disabilities. *Admission* free, programmes vary. *Open* daily 10am–5pm.

NEW ZEALAND ACADEMY OF FINE ARTS

Ground Floor, Wharf Offices, 1 Queens Wharf, tel 499-8807, www.nzafa.com

Housed in the historic Wharf Offices, the New Zealand Academy of Fine Arts (established in 1882) presents a range of stimulating artwork from all over the country. Most works are for sale at a low rate of commission, thereby offering support to the Academy's members, artists and craftspeople across New Zealand. *Admission* free. *Open* daily 10am–5pm.

NEW ZEALAND PORTRAIT GALLERY – TE PUKENGA WHAKAATA

Bowen House, corner Lambton Quay & Bowen Street, tel 472-8874, www.nzportgal.org.nz

See New Zealanders through the perceptive eyes of painters, caricaturists, sculptors and photographers. A place of discovery, the gallery presents the images and stories of New Zealanders who have shaped the country's identity. *Admission* free. *Open* Mon–Fri 10am–4pm, Sat 10am–1pm.

ENJOY PUBLIC ART GALLERY

Level One, 174 Cuba Street, tel 384-0174, www.enjoy.org.nz

Enjoy is funded predominantly by Creative New Zealand to present the work of both emerging and established artists. Enjoy focuses on installational conceptual art that responds to the space of the gallery as a particular location and cultural framework, and actively promotes critical dialogue surrounding contemporary art-making. *Admission* free. *Open* Wed–Fri 12pm–6pm, Sat/Sun 12pm–5pm.

NEW ZEALAND PARLIAMENT BUILDINGS

Corner Lambton Quay & Molesworth Streets, tel 471-9503,
www.ps.parliament.govt.nz

Visit our beautifully refurbished Parliament Buildings with lovely
lawn out front. Parliament has met on its present site in Wellington
since 1865, when it moved from Auckland. The buildings have
changed over time and you can see this history in their architecture:
the Edwardian neo-classical *Parliament House*, the Victorian Gothic
Parliamentary Library and the unique 1970s *Beehive*. The information
desk in the middle building offers advice, hourly guided tours,
video viewing, a souvenir shop and changing historic displays.
Learn about the restoration, view artwork including remarkable
Maori weaving and carving, picnic in the gardens and see statues
and plaques. Watch politicians in action while the House is sitting.
Admission free. *Open* Mon–Fri 9am–5pm, Sat 9.30am–4pm, Sun
11.30am–4pm. Guided one-hour tours leave on the hour Mon–Fri
10am–4pm, Sat 10am–3pm, Sun 12pm–3pm.

COLONIAL COTTAGE MUSEUM

68 Nairn Street, Mt Cook, tel 384-9122, www.colonialcottagemuseum.co.nz

Wellington's oldest identified building, built as a family home by
English immigrant William Wallis in 1858 who lived there with his
wife and 10 children. The cottage retells the story of family life in
colonial Wellington; a time when nails were still imported into
the country and candles were made from meat fat. Displays show
the ways in which the first colonials blended their lives from their
Victorian homeland with the dictates of a new country. Within
walking distance of downtown Wellington, and the start point for
the **Aro Valley Heritage Trail** (see CITY WALKS). Gift shop and parking.
Admission adult $5, child with parents free. *Open* (Boxing Day–30
April) daily 12pm–4pm; (1 May–24 Dec) Wed–Sun 12pm–4pm.

ADAM ART GALLERY – TE PATAKA TOI

Gate 3, Victoria University, Kelburn Parade, tel 463-5489, www.vuw.ac.nz

The only purpose-built university gallery in New Zealand; open and
free to all. Exhibitions present and critically interpret visual art,
craft, architecture and design. *Admission* by koha (donation). *Open*
Tues–Sun 11am–5pm, closed public hols and between exhibitions.

MAORI TREASURES

56–58 Guthrie Street, Waiwhetu, Lower Hutt, tel 939-9630,
www.maori-treasures.com

Discover a treasured Maori art tradition that spans three centuries
and enjoy hands-on activities, demonstrations and exhibits in
the private studios of a family of renowned Maori artists. You'll
be warmly welcomed, and amazed by the stunning artwork being
created in front of your eyes. Tours run every weekday, and there's
authentic, quality Maori art and craft in the gift shop, and a café
on site. This is a short journey from the city well worth making.
Admission by enquiry. *Open* Mon–Sat 9am–4pm (closed 22 Dec–6 Jan).

NATIONAL TATTOO MUSEUM

42 Abel Smith Street, tel 385-6444, www.mokomuseum.org.nz

The public face of a charitable trust, established to provide a forum
for the sharing and protection of tattoo/ta moko. Their vision:
'global unity for tattooed and non-tattooed people alike … to treat
every culture with the utmost respect, document and display their
individual stories as accurately and honestly as possible while
continuing to evolve with the Art of Tattoo'. Traditional Maori
tattoo, ta moko, is one of the arts by which this country is best
known overseas, and ranks as one of the most sophisticated, highly
developed tattoo traditions anywhere in the world. The museum
houses the *Aotearoa Artists Gallery*, hosting bi-monthly local, national
and international exhibitions. *Admission* adult $5, child (under 16) $2,
infant (under 5) free. *Open* Tues–Sat 12pm–5.30pm.

NATIONAL CRICKET MUSEUM

Old Stand, Basin Reserve, tel 385-6602

This fine collection of artefacts chronicles New Zealand's
progression over the past century to its status as a world-class
cricketing nation. Its home, the **Basin Reserve**, was supposed to be a
shipping basin with Kent and Cambridge Terraces the parallel canals
leading to it. However, the 1855 earthquake raised the land and
drained an extensive marsh, and the basin became a cricket ground
instead. A much better idea! *Admission* adult $3, child $1. *Open* (mid-
Nov–31 Mar) daily 10.30am–3.30pm, extended on match days; (rest
of year) Sat/Sun only 10.30am–3.30pm, or by arrangement.

DOWSE ART MUSEUM

35 Laings Road, Lower Hutt, tel 570-6500,
www.huttcity.govt.nz/council/services/recreation/dowse

The Dowse enjoys an excellent reputation for presenting innovative exhibitions focused on New Zealand art, craft and design. Delivered in surprising ways and enhanced with performance and hands-on activities, find out why it's frequently changing programme amazes and delights visitors. Popular café on site. Get to the Dowse on the no. 83 bus from Wellington City; by car it will take you 15 minutes (follow the signs from the Petone off-ramp). *Admission* free (except for major touring exhibitions). *Open* Mon–Fri 10am–4pm, Sat/Sun 11am–5pm.

PETONE SETTLERS MUSEUM

The Esplanade, Petone, tel 568-8373,
www.huttcity.govt.nz/council/services/recreation/settlers

This museum is proof that you needn't be big to be good. The focus of *The Story House* is the migration and settlement of the Wellington and Hutt Valley region and the social history of the lower Hutt Valley. Multimedia databases include records of passenger ship lists/family histories (Wellington arrivals 1840–97) and Hutt Valley housing. Interactive exhibits and a walk-through forest take visitors on a journey through the Lower Hutt Valley's past, present and future. *Admission* by donation. *Open* Tues–Fri 12pm–4pm, Sat/Sun 1pm–5pm.

PATAKA – PORIRUA MUSEUM OF ARTS AND CULTURES

Corner Norrie & Parumoana Streets, Porirua, tel 237-1511,
www.pataka.org.nz

A museum, art gallery and library, Pataka showcases leading contemporary Maori, Pacific Island and New Zealand artists and reflects the social and cultural heritage of Porirua City. The *Melody Farm* displays a collection of pianolas, organs, phonographs and musical rarities from 1840–60. Pataka has a superb Japanese garden, a café and an early-times courtyard, and is also home to *Whitireia Performing Arts School* and *Porirua City Library*. *Admission* free to galleries; Melody Farm adult $3.50, child $2, infant free. *Open* Mon–Sat 10am–4.30pm, Sun 11am–4.30pm.

Street Art and Architecture

Wellington's inner city is vibrant and diverse, and will be much enjoyed by those who appreciate a fine building, a fascinating sculpture or brilliant mural.

Early on, fire and earthquake destroyed many colonial buildings, so you'll see only a few dating back to the mid 1850s. In 1865, Wellington became the capital, and the following two decades saw a government building boom. Fortunately, the highlight of this era has been preserved and opened to the public. As the twentieth century began, Wellington's port prospered, and many fine wharf buildings of this period remain, as do several ornate Victorian banking chambers. The advent of steel framing around 1910 led to taller buildings with greater earthquake resistance. There was no suitable local stone for building (although bricks were made from local clay), but you will see plenty of granite and marble from other parts of the country. The 1930s saw a remarkable flourish of art deco of which many examples survive. Outer claddings were applied in the 1950s and 60s giving Wellington's modern buildings the international look we see today.

The art deco Prudential Assurance building, shortly after its completion in 1934.

Gordon Burt Collection, Alexander Turnbull Library, Wellington, New Zealand, PAColl-4118.

Recent times have seen a wider appreciation of Wellington's heritage. Many citizens have fought and continue to fight for the preservation of our historic places, while artists and visionaries enrich our public spaces through their street art and architecture.

Our city today offers much to those who care to cast their eager eye around, inward and upward. We bring you here merely some highlights, and a few ways to find out more.

The best way to explore Wellington's city art and architecture is by following one of many *heritage trails*, interpretative maps for which are available from the Visitor Information Centre and similar outlets. The CITY WALKS section has details on these.

In the middle of town, **Civic Square**, the city's meeting place, is a little over a decade old. The distinctive *nikau palms* around the perimeter were designed by local architect Ian Athfield, as was the *Wellington City Library* (1991) bordering the square. Alongside, the *City Gallery* resides in the old library (1939). The terracotta paving is laid in the form of Maui's line, *Te Aho a Maui*, that he used to fish up the North Island. The silver globe is Neil Dawson's *Ferns*, representing five varieties of native fern. It may look lighter than air, but actually weighs 175 kg! There are numerous other sculptures in and around the square. The **City to Sea Bridge** sculptures by Maori artist Para Matchitt evoke stories of the sea, land, navigation and arrival.

Over the bridge and on to the **waterfront** with its old wharf buildings and the *Writers Walk* (see LITERARY AND LIBRARY). The landmark of the promenade is *Te Papa*, the biggest building project in the city's history, completed in 1998, and described by its architects as 'a high intensity roller-coaster architectural adventure'. Standing proud alongside the boating club is *The Coming of the Maori*, sculptured in plaster by William Trethewey for the 1940 Centennial Exhibition. This fine sculpture depicts the great Maori explorer *Kupe*, legendary tenth century discoverer of Aotearoa, with his wife Hine Te Aparangi and magician Peka-Hourangi in their canoe *Matahoua*. The sculpture lay badly damaged in storage for many years until dusted off by concerned citizens. It was cast in bronze and installed here in 2000. Behind Kupe you can see the *Odlins Building* (1907) undergoing major renovation. **Frank Kitts Park**, back towards the port, has various sculptures and memorials dotted about, including the *Wahine mast* (see page 52 for more on the *Wahine*).

The **Lambton Quay** area has some of the best buildings in town. The striking art deco *Prudential Assurance Building* (1934) at 332 Lambton Quay was the skyscraper of its day, and the first in town to be framed with steel. Check out the detail. The *Public Trust Building* (1909) at 131 Lambton Quay is the city's best example of Edwardian baroque. As you walk along the quay, look out for a series of modern sculptures: *Protoplasm* (Lambton/Hunter corner), *Invisible City* (Lambton/Grey corner) *Nga Korerorero* (Midland Park), *Shells* (Lambton/Waring Taylor corner), *Spinning Top* (top of Woodward) and *Starfish* (Waring Taylor/Featherston corner).

Government Buildings, as drawn by Lewis E. Martin.

From Buildings to Enjoy, Dunmore Press, Palmerston North (1995).

Wellington's architectural **must see** is the *Government Buildings* opposite the *Beehive*. Completed in 1876 and carefully restored in the 1990s, this is the largest wooden building in the Southern Hemisphere and among the finest examples of New Zealand's architectural heritage. Built to look like stone, it boasts imposing façades, sweeping staircases, cast-iron fireplaces and kauri-clad interiors. Now home to Victoria University's law faculty, the building is open to the public, with a self-guided tour on offer (*admission* free; *open* Mon–Fri 9am–4.30pm, Sat 10am–3pm).

There are many more nineteenth century buildings in **Thorndon**. *Old St Paul's Church* (1866) at 34 Mulgrave Street is a unique example of Colonial Gothic architecture. Constructed entirely of native timber, the warm wooden interior is enhanced with magnificent stained-glass windows (*admission* by donation; *open* daily). A ramble around Hobson Street and the Tinakori Lanes will reward walkers with many more early buildings, mostly residential.

The **Botanic Garden** boasts six sculptures including, for Henry Moore fans, *Bronze Form* situated on the Salamanca Lawn. *Rudderstone* by Denis O'Connor is another highlight.

Cuba Street has many buildings built during the late 1800s and early 1900s, and one of the most imposing is the *Watkins Building* (1904) at 176 Cuba Street. The largest Edwardian commercial building in the area, this prominent landmark has recently undergone renovation and earthquake strengthening.

The **can't miss** of Cuba Street is the *Bucket Fountain*. Architect Graham Allardice designed it in celebration of the first pedestrian mall in New Zealand, but it was much reviled when first installed. It was not expected to survive, but a contrary public protested wildly when the city council suggested removing it some years later. Recently, a certain movie star boasted that he mistook it for a urinal. He thought that was funny. We don't; even hobbits must respect the buckets.

Positively Wellington Tourism (Nick Servian)

The most interesting buildings at the **Courtenay Place** end of town are the theatres, all of which are best enjoyed inside with ice cream (see DRAMA, DANCE AND CONCERTS, and CINEMA). Well worth a look in this vicinity though is the mural at *Il Casino* on Tory Street and, just around the corner, *Forest and Bird* on Taranaki Street. There are many other fine murals, so keep your eyes peeled.

If you're heading to the **airport/Miramar**, look out for two wind sculptures: *Zephyrometer* (Phil Price) near the Cobham Drive/Evans Bay Parade corner, and *Pacific Grass* (Kon Dimopoulos) on the Cobham Drive/Calabar Road roundabout.

FOR MORE INFORMATION ...

New Zealand Historic Places Trust – Pouhere Taonga

(www.historic.org.nz) The country's leading protector of culturally significant sites and buildings. Their heritage trail booklet *Historic Wellington* details 29 notable sites in the city.

Wellington Sculpture Trust

(www.sculpture.org.nz) The Sculpture Trust commissions contemporary public sculpture 'to support the creative arts in New Zealand and to enhance the cityscape and lifestyle of Wellington'.

Tareitanga Sculpture Symposium

(www.tareitanga.org.nz) A biennial event, next held Jan/Feb 2005. Scores of local and international artists meet for a month on the waterfront to sculpt works in limestone and marble.

Literary and Library

NATIONAL LIBRARY – TE PUNA MATAURANGA O AOTEAROA
58–78 Molesworth Street, tel 474-3000, www.natlib.govt.nz
One of the country's leading cultural and information centres, holding rich and varied collections including the *Family History Collection* where visitors can research their genealogy. It also houses the world-famous **Alexander Turnbull Library**, a 'library within a library' specialising in documentary materials – books, manuscripts, photographs, drawings and prints, music, newspapers, maps and oral histories. The *Gallery* exhibits works mostly from the library's heritage collections and also runs a lively events programme. Shop and café on site. Guided tours of exhibitions by arrangement. *Admission* free. *Open* library: Mon–Fri 9am–5pm, Sat 9am–1pm; gallery: Mon–Fri 9am–5pm, Sat 9am–4.30pm, Sun 1pm–4.30pm.

ARCHIVES NEW ZEALAND – TE WHARE TOHU TUHITUHINGA
10 Mulgrave Street, Thorndon, tel 499-5595, www.archives.govt.nz
Archives New Zealand is the country's largest repository of non-current official records concerning New Zealand's history and development. The original *Treaty of Waitangi* and the 1893 *Women's Suffrage Petition* are among the important documents on permanent display in the **Constitution Room** – both can be found on Unesco's World Heritage List. Other galleries have changing exhibitions on a variety of historical and cultural topics. The *Reading Room* provides free access for researchers to all records held. Café on site. *Admission* free. *Open* Mon–Fri 9am–5pm, Sat 9m–1pm.

WELLINGTON CITY LIBRARY – TE MATAPIHI O TE AO NUI
Civic Square, tel 801-4040, www.wcl.govt.nz
One of New Zealand's most exciting buildings, the library not only houses a fabulous collection of books and music but also represents a unique architectural style, fantastic both inside and out. Check out the copper and steel nikau palms. The foyer has useful visitor information such as bus timetables and event flyers, and the mezzanine *Clarks* café is recommended. *Admission* free. *Open* Mon–Thurs 9.30am–8.30pm, Fri 9.30am–9pm, Sat 9.30am–5pm, Sun 1pm–4pm.

Wellington Writers and their Books

The Wellington literary community continues its long tradition of producing many fine writers, publishers and books. Here we bring you a few well-known names and books of note. Local booksellers will be happy to help you find them (see SHOPPING).

For a good background on Wellington writing, we recommend *Wellington: The City in Literature* edited by **Kate Camp**, an anthology of fiction and poetry. It includes the work of Wellington's most famous author, **Katherine Mansfield** (1888–1923), who lived here until she left for the lights of London in the early 1900s. You can learn more about her at the Katherine Mansfield Birthplace (see opposite).

Celebrated contemporary novelists include **Patricia Grace**, a fore-runner of modern Maori literature, **Dame Fiona Kidman**, **Maurice Gee**, **Marilyn Duckworth**, **Barbara Anderson**, **Lloyd Jones** and **Barbara Else**.

A recent national ranking of our best young authors placed Wellingtonian **Catherine Chidgey** at number one, with other locals **Damien Wilkins**, **Kate Duignan** and **Tim Corballis** featuring too. Also named was **Elizabeth Knox**, internationally acclaimed novelist and author of *The Vintner's Luck* and *Daylight*, winner of New Zealand's premiere fiction award in 1999. Ms Knox is published by *Victoria University Press*, acclaimed for its production of quality novels, many of them debuts for developing authors.

If you enjoy poetry, your first port of call should be the deservedly popular *Big Weather: Poems of Wellington* selected by Gregory O'Brien and Louise White. A 'composite portrait of Wellington and a celebration of its bustling creative life', this lovely little anthology is from *Mallinson Rendel*, a local publisher whose **Hairy Maclary** children's books are favourites for children both home and abroad. *Big Weather* features contributions from many leading local poets: **Jenny Bornholdt, Kate Camp, Lauris Edmond, Alistair Te Ariki Campbell, Denis Glover, Bill Manhire, Vincent O'Sullivan, Vivienne Plumb, Roma Potiki, Anne Powell, Harry Ricketts, Bill Sewell, J.C. Sturm, Jo Thorpe** and **Louise Wrightson**.

There are several good illustrated histories currently available including *Gavid McLean's* **Wellington: The First Years of European Settlement 1840–1850**, a fascinating account of the city's formative years. **Magnitude Eight Plus** by *Rodney Grapes* focuses on the 1855 Wellington earthquake, the largest in New Zealand history. **Wellington: A Capital Century** by *David McGill* is a bumper book, packed with illustrations that tell the story of the last 100 years. The stories of Maori urban migrants are told in **The Silent Migration: Ngati Poneke Young Maori Club 1937–1948**, edited by *Jonathon Dennis, Patricia Grace* and *Irihapeti Ramsden*. The city's natural history is explored in *Winsome Shepherd's* pleasing **Wellington's Heritage: Plants, Gardens, and Landscapes**.

Souvenir books to take home and remember us by include the pretty little **Wildflower City** by *Alan Knowles* and *Colin Webb*; **Wellington and Beyond**, photography by *Rob Suisted*; **Why go to the Riviera: Images of Wellington** by *Peter Shaw*; and **Capital Perspective: Wellington in Miniature** by *Hilary Tipping*.

For more information about New Zealand books and writers visit **www.bookcouncil.org.nz**, and to buy New Zealand books from overseas, we recommend **www.nzbooksabroad.com**.

KATHERINE MANSFIELD BIRTHPLACE – TE PUAKITANGA

25 Tinakori Road, Thorndon, tel 473-7268
Step back into Victorian New Zealand at the 1888 birthplace of Kathleen Mansfield Beauchamp, New Zealand's most famous author and one of the world's best-known short story writers. This exquisitely restored house and heritage garden provide an essential background to Mansfield's writing and an opportunity to experience New Zealand society of the time. Gift shop and teas. *Admission* adult $5.50, student $4, child $2. *Open* daily 10am–4pm.

WELLINGTON WRITERS WALK

Waterfront between Chaffers Marina, City to Sea Bridge & Frank Kitts Park
The Writers Walk consists of 11 text sculptures located along the waterfront, each one containing a quotation about the city from one of the many writers who have, at some time, made Wellington their home. Such writers are Katherine Mansfield, Denis Glover, James K. Baxter, Bruce Mason, Lauris Edmond, Maurice Gee and Patricia Grace. A free booklet, available from the *Visitor Information Centre*, has a map and further information.

Drama, Dance and Concerts

There is plenty of live performance in Wellington, the home of the national orchestra, ballet and opera as well as many other professional and amateur performance groups. So expect to be spoilt for choice.

The renowned biennial *New Zealand Festival* and its *Fringe* occur in the even years (2004/2006), bringing a huge range of international, national and local talent to the fore (**www.nzfestival.telecom.co.nz**). There are scores of other performance festivals and events, many of which are listed in the EVENTS CALENDAR. Show listings can be found daily in the *Dominion Post*, the weekly *Capital Times* and individual websites as detailed below.

Tickets are available at most venues. The *Visitor Information Centre* sells reduced price tickets for Circa, Downstage and Bats after 12pm on the day of performance on a first-come-first-served basis. **Ticketek** booths are located at the *Michael Fowler Centre* and the *St James Theatre* – they ticket many, but not all events.

For more live music, see PUBS, BARS AND LIVE MUSIC.

CIRCA THEATRE
Next to Te Papa, 1 Taranaki Street, tel 801-7992, www.circa.co.nz
Award-winning Circa Theatre is considered one of New Zealand's liveliest and most innovative professional theatres, spectacularly located on the waterfront. Showcasing international and New Zealand drama, comedies and musicals, Circa has helped foster the careers of some of New Zealand's best-known theatre professionals. There are two theatres, one accommodating 240 seats and the other a 100-seat studio. Performances are held daily from Tues–Sun. The *Café & Bar* is open at show times. *Bookings* can be made by phone, via the website or from the box office at the theatre. Door sales available one hour before performance. *Tickets* $16–$30.

DOWNSTAGE THEATRE
12 Cambridge Terrace, tel 801-6946, www.downstage.co.nz
Downstage is New Zealand's longest-running professional theatre, entertaining audiences for almost 40 years. An intimate 250-seat venue, Downstage delivers top quality, dynamic live theatre. Many

landmark New Zealand plays have been premiered at Downstage, and it has *'long been an important part of Wellington's, and New Zealand's, cultural fabric'*, according to Prime Minister Helen Clark. Performances Mon–Tues 6.30pm, Wed–Sat 8pm. *Bookings* can be made by phone, via the website or from the box office at the theatre. *Tickets $15–$35.*

BATS THEATRE
1 Kent Terrace, tel 802-4175, www.bats.co.nz
For a truly Wellington theatre experience, go to BATS. Now in its 15th year, BATS' founding philosophy was to rekindle the popularity and accessibility of theatre for young people, and to provide a 'way in' for young artists. That means you get a varied programme of a consistently high standard, very reasonably priced. BATS is also a key venue for the *Wellington Fringe Festival* and *The Laugh! Festival*. *Bookings* can be made by phone, email bats@bats.co.nz or in person at the box office, open two hours before each show. Door sales available. *Tickets $10–$18.*

ST JAMES THEATRE
77–87 Courtenay Place, www.stjames.co.nz
New Zealand's finest Edwardian lyric theatre, this 1912 building faced demolition in the mid 1980s, until rescued by the people of Wellington. Fundraising began in 1993, and the $20 million restoration job was completed in 1998. The theatre now proudly boasts opera, dance and major musical shows, and is home to the *Royal New Zealand Ballet*. The atmospheric foyer houses the *Jimmy Café & Bar* serving light meals and coffee during the day, as well as full dining facilities pre-show. *Ticketek* box office located inside.

THE OPERA HOUSE
111–113 Manners Street, www.stjames.co.nz
The Grand Old Lady of Wellington is a splendid lyric theatre and a wonderful example of early 1900s architecture. A venue for contemporary dance, comedy, community shows and smaller touring productions, the theatre has been progressively refurbished inside and out over the last three years. The *Opera House Espresso Bar* serves coffee and light refreshments at show time.

NEW ZEALAND STRING QUARTET
www.nzsq.co.nz, tel 499-8883
New Zealand's premier chamber music ensemble performs a wide repertoire both at home and abroad.

CHAMBER MUSIC NEW ZEALAND
www.chambermusic.co.nz, tel 0800-266-2378
Presents international chamber music events at *Wellington Town Hall*.

WELLINGTON CHAMBER MUSIC SOCIETY
A wide-ranging programme of Sunday afternoon concerts. Bookings from *Ticketek*.

WELLINGTON SINFONIA
www.wellingtonsinfonia.co.nz, tel 801-3882
The busy and versatile orchestra of central New Zealand, performing opera and ballet, silent movie scores and huge community concerts.

Other venues you may need to know ...

Michael Fowler Centre
111 Wakefield Street, www.wellingtonconventioncentre.com
Home of the NZSO and venue for many other events.

Wellington Town Hall
Next to the Michael Fowler Centre, Wakefield Street
www.wellingtonconventioncentre.com
Lovely 1904 hall, used for smaller concerts and shows.

Queens Wharf Events Centre
Jervois Quay, www.wellingtonconventioncentre.com
Host to large concerts, exhibitions, trade shows and sporting events.

Overseas Terminal
Chaffers Marina, Herd Street, www.overseasterminal.co.nz
Large exhibitions, conferences and occasional rug auctions.

The Parthenon
5 Hania Street, Mt Victoria (off Pirie Street)
This classic, intimate venue has a great dance floor, and is used mainly for festival shows and some good gigs.

NBR NEW ZEALAND OPERA

www.nzopera.com, tel 499-8343

New Zealand's premier opera company presents several seasons each year at Wellington's grandest venue, the *St James Theatre*, where good seats are reasonably priced. Renowned for its quality productions, each opera season features a mix of well-known opera favourites alongside less familiar works, with a top line-up of international and New Zealand singers, conductors, directors and musicians. A night at the opera comes highly recommended. Visit the website for season details, ticket prices and bookings.

ROYAL NEW ZEALAND BALLET

www.nzballet.org.nz

The Royal New Zealand Ballet performs throughout New Zealand and overseas. Their repertoire is eclectic, from nineteenth century classics to twenty first century contemporary works. Danish Royal Ballet Principal Dancer Poul Gnatt formed the RNZB in 1953. In the pioneering days, dancers performed night in night out, as well as unloaded and repacked the set, rigged the lights and ironed the costumes, with the local community providing accommodation. That spirit survives today, with a loyal New Zealand public very much enjoying the opportunity to see professional ballet in their town. Wellington's *St James Theatre* is home to the RNZB, with information and bookings available from *Ticketek* or by visiting their website.

NEW ZEALAND SYMPHONY ORCHESTRA

www.nzso.co.nz, tel 0800-479-674

Our national orchestra enjoys a lively profile both inside and outside New Zealand. Performances in well-filled halls are testament to their developing reputation, as is their involvement in opera and ballet productions, television, radio and film (including *The Lord of the Rings*). The NZSO gave its first public performance in March 1947. Today they play more than 100 performances each year including seasons of major symphonic repertoire in seven centres and a wide range of special programmes. The *Chamber Orchestra* and *National Youth Orchestra* are part of the family. The orchestra's Wellington concerts are usually held at their home, the *Michael Fowler Centre*, with bookings available from *Ticketek*.

Cinema

Welcome to *Wellywood*, *Middle-earth*, home of the world premiere of Peter Jackson's *Lord of the Rings: The Return of the King*. Peter loves the movies, and so do we; we've got the cinemas, filmmakers and festivals to prove it. If you're hanging around, why not join the *Wellington Film Society* (filmsociety.wellington.net.nz, PO Box 1584).

FILM FESTIVAL CALENDAR

Feb/Mar   **Drifting Clouds Short Film Festival** www.driftingcloudsfilmfest.com
A one-night screening of short films under the stars.

April   **World Cinema Showcase**, www.wellington.nzff.co.nz
An annual Autumn season of film featuring New Zealand premieres of international festival hits, stimulating documentaries and new prints of Hollywood classics.

Latin American Film Festival, www.paramount.co.nz
An annual showcase of Latin American film supported by the embassies in Wellington of Argentina, Brazil, Chile, Mexico and Peru.

June   **Out Takes Lesbian and Gay Film Festival**, www.outtakes.org.nz
The best recent queer cinema from home and abroad.

Jun/Jul   **Becks Incredible Film Festival**, www.becksincrediblefilmfest.co.nz
Arcane, controversial, subversive, insane, thrilling, odd, cheesy and sexy – from the farthest reaches of the planet.

July   **Wellington Fringe Film Festival**, www.fringefilmfest.co.nz
Includes short film programme and music clip awards.

Wellington Film Festival, www.wellington.nzff.co.nz
Three weeks of movie madness, and the highlight of the year. Well over a hundred films played to huge, hungry audiences, all over town.

Sept   **Middle Eastern Film Festival**, www.paramount.co.nz
Two weeks of feature and documentary films contributing to an awareness of Middle Eastern cultures, histories and arts.

Oct   **Italian Film Festival**, www.italianfilmfestival.co.nz
The annual showcase of Italian film, presented in association with the Italian Embassy.

The Lord of The Rings: Made in New Zealand

The epic film triology, *The Lord of The Rings*, based on the books by J. R. R. Tolkien, was made in New Zealand by Wellington based Three Foot Six with the help of Weta Digital and the Weta Workshop.

Filming started in Wellington's town belt in October 1999, with *The Fellowship of the Ring* released in December 2001, *The Two Towers* in December 2002, and the final instalment *The Return of the King* in December 2003, thus completing the trilogy.

The films' director is local filmmaking hero, Peter Jackson, whose previous film credits include *Bad Taste* (1987), *Meet the Feebles* (1989), *Brain Dead* (1992), *Heavenly Creatures* (1994), *Forgotten Silver* (1995) and *The Frighteners* (1996). Peter has made cinematic history as the first director to ever make three major feature films simultaneously.

The star-studded cast includes Elijah Wood, Sir Ian Holm, Liv Tyler, Sean Bean, Orlando Bloom, Cate Blanchett, Viggo Mortensen and Sir Ian McKellen, all of whom were reported to have enjoyed their time in Wellywood. 'I look back on it all with enormous pleasure,' said McKellen. The crew numbered over 2500 people, which offers some account of the huge budget, rumoured to be NZ$650 million.

Many of the films' 100 locations were in the Wellington region, including *Rivendell* and the *Fords of Isen*. Ian Brodie's excellent *Lord of The Rings Location Guidebook* can help you find them all.

On 1 December 2003, Wellington proudly hosted the world premiere of the third film, *The Return of the King*. Mark Ordesky of the films' production company, New Line Cinema, announced: 'I can't think of a better way to celebrate the final chapter of this epic trilogy than to have the world premiere in the very city and country that has made these films unique.'

Sources: Dominion Post, www.lordoftherings.net

EMBASSY THEATRE

10 Kent Terrace, tel 384-7657, www.deluxe.co.nz

Built in 1924, the Embassy has just undergone a major renovation timed to be ready for the world premiere of *The Lord of the Rings: The Return of the King*. New Zealand's grandest picture palace sits proudly overlooking Wellington's entertainment precinct. With a giant cinemascope screen and state of the art digital sound, the 750 seat Embassy offers a world-class Wellington cinema experience.

PARAMOUNT THEATRE

25 Courtenay Place, tel 384-4080, www.deluxe.co.nz

Opened in 1917, the Paramount is Wellington's oldest surviving cinema, refurbished in a distinctly European style. It offers a varied programme of quality films, and is the host of several fantastic film festivals. A lovely theatre with quality coffee, beer and ice cream, the Paramount deserves its loyal local following.

PENTHOUSE CINEMA AND CAFÉ

205 Ohiro Road, Brooklyn, tel 384-3157, www.penthousecinema.co.nz

The charming Penthouse, so named because it sits upon Brooklyn hill, is well known for its stunning art deco architecture and the screening of quality films. It originally opened as the Vogue in 1939, and has been owned by Kisby family since 1975. The Penthouse has an intimate and relaxed atmosphere, a café on site, and a stylish foyer for loitering. Telephone bookings accepted; disabled access.

LIGHT HOUSE CINEMA

52 Beach Street, Petone, tel 939-2061, www.lighthousecinema.co.nz

Local theatre with excellent quality picture and sound, two-seater sofas and bar facilities.

ARO STREET VIDEO SHOP

97 Aro Street, Aro Valley, tel 801-7101, www.arovideo.co.nz

A first-rate independent video rental store, and a key destination for those with a serious interest in cinema. Covering a world and a century of moving images, this is a brilliant library of over 8000 hand picked titles, nestled in the heart of Wellington's 'bohemian' district, Aro Valley. Open daily 10am–10pm.

THE NEW ZEALAND FILM ARCHIVE – TE ANAKURA WHITIAHUA

Corner Ghuznee & Taranaki Streets, tel 384-7647, www.filmarchive.org.nz

The Film Archive is the country's premier moving image heritage centre, etablished in 1981. The Archive's commitment is to collect, protect and project New Zealand's film and television history. The *Film Archive Mediaplex*, opening April 2004, has an extensive reference library, research centre, screenings and special events, with an on-site cinema, café, gallery and information centre with Internet access. Enquire for opening hours.

ATTRACTIONS

City Lookouts

THE CABLE CAR

Cable Car Lane, 280 Lambton Quay, tel 472-2199, www.cablecarmuseum.co.nz
Deservedly one of Wellington's most popular attractions, the cable car runs from Lambton Quay to the lookout at the top of the **Botanic Garden** via Clifton Terrace, Talavera, Salamanca and Kelburn Park. At the top, a classic city view takes in the city's central business district and Mt Victoria, across the harbour to Eastbourne, the Hutt Valley and spectacular peaks beyond. The **Cable Car Museum** (see MUSEUMS) is next to the lookout. From here, either return via the cable car or preferably walk back down through the gorgeous gardens taking in the **Carter Observatory** or the historic **Bolton Street Memorial Park** as you go. You'll emerge across the road from Parliament. *Tickets* adult $1.80, child $1, family $10. *Cars run* every 10 minutes Mon–Fri 7am–10pm, Sat 8.30am–10pm, Sun 9am–10pm.

MOUNT VICTORIA LOOKOUT

Via Thane Road or Alexandra Road, Roseneath
A 360° bird's eye view giving a particularly good grasp of the harbour shape and size. The lookout is an hour's walk from Courtenay Place, and a pleasant circuit can be had if you walk along Oriental Parade, head up the hill via the **Southern Walkway** to the top, and come down via any route on the city side of the hill (just follow your nose). At the summit of Mt Victoria you'll find the lookout, built from surplus stone and marble from a demolished London bridge. The triangular memorial is dedicated to Antarctic explorer Admiral Richard E. Byrd, the first person to fly over the South Pole, and sometime visitor to Wellington. Local potter Doreen Blumhardt created the memorial from 2500 tiles to depict *Aurora Australis*.

WIND TURBINE

Off Ashton Fitchett Drive, Brooklyn
Stand under a whirling turbine and take in wonderful views of the Wellington region, Cook Strait and the South Island. This is New Zealand's first commercially viable wind turbine generator, completed in 1993. In 1989, wind activity was evaluated at 17 sites, and Wellington was found to have 'higher than normal' wind

patterns, making it an ideal site for a turbine experiment. This 32-metre high, 23-tonne turbine outputs a maximum 225 kilowatts, enough electricity for 60–80 homes. It's built to survive winds of 200 km/hr, but automatically shuts down at over 80 km/hr. With wind in abundance, the Wellington region may well see more turbines in the future. But enough about the turbine; isn't this a glorious view? The no. 7 bus to Kowhai Park will get you closest.

WRIGHTS HILL LOOKOUT

Wrights Hill, Karori, tel 476-8593

The lookout is the highpoint of a recreation reserve that offers expansive views, picnic spots and bush walks. The reserve is home to *Wrights Hill Fortress*, an historic gun emplacement, and 620 metres of underground tunnels constructed during World War II for an invasion that never came. The guns were tested twice though, shattering local windows. The fortress is open to the public four times a year, with the local restoration society giving interesting tours of the facility. Followed by a stroll and a sizzled sausage, this makes a lovely public holiday outing for the whole family. The reserve is accessible all year round, free. *Admission* to fortress adult $5, child $3, family $12. *Open* Waitangi Day (Feb 6), Anzac Day (April 25), Queens Birthday (early June) and Labour Day (late Oct), 10am–4pm. Private tours by arrangement. The Karori West no. 12 bus will get you closest (Mon–Fri only) or take the frequent Karori Park, also no. 12, and walk from the Karori Mall up Campbell Street (around half an hour, uphill). A more ambitious access route is walking or biking the *Karori Sanctuary fenceline* (see MOUNTAIN BIKING).

MASSEY MEMORIAL

Point Halswell, car park on Massey Road, Miramar

They don't make 'em like this any more! This grand memorial, dedicated to *William Ferguson Massey* (New Zealand prime minister 1912–25) is perched on the point originally known to Maori as *Kaitawharo* ('to eat jellyfish'). The area was renamed in the 1840s after Edmond Halswell, Commissioner of Native Reserves. In 1886, fears of a Russian invasion following the Crimean War led to the construction of a gun emplacement on this site, but shortly after Massey's death in 1925, this site was allocated for his burial.

The memorial is made of Coromandel granite covered with Kairuru marble from Takaka. Described by some as ostentatious, and some as folly, we prefer magnificent. The vantage point offers a unique view of the city and harbour, and delightful picnicking on a summer day.

The unveiling ceremony of Massey Memorial, conducted by His Excellency the Governor-General, Lord Bledisloe, on 19 September 1930.

Alexander Turnbull Library, Wellington, New Zealand, F-711-1/1.

MT KAU KAU SUMMIT

An hour's walk (probably less) will reward you with one of most breathtaking views of the Wellington region. The walk starts at **Khandallah Park** (Woodmancote Road) and takes you through century-old native plant regeneration. It's not a particularly strenuous climb, with plenty of places to stop and rest. Towards the summit, thinned native vegetation is interspersed with exotics, particularly pines and macrocarpas. The walkway reaches farmland at an altitude of about 430 metres, and there you'll see the big tower and the lookout. To the east is the dramatic panorama of the city, harbour and the *Rimutaka Range*, while to the north the *Tararua Ranges* dominate the skyline (if you can see their peaks, you picked a grand day indeed!). The South Island will be clearly visible to the south on all but the murkiest days, and chances are you'll see snow-capped *Mt Tapuae-o-Uenuku*, the 2885 m pinnacle of the Kaikoura Ranges. This walk meets up with the **Northern Walkway** (see CITY WALKS). Transport to the park is via train Mon–Sat, or daily by bus. Call *Ridewell* for information on 801–7000. If you like this walk, you'll love the *Belmont Trig* (see SCENIC RESERVES).

Gardens, Parks and Playgrounds

WELLINGTON BOTANIC GARDEN

101 Glenmore Street, Thorndon, tel 499-1903, www.wellington.govt.nz

In 1843, the town council leased 13 acres of land to the Horticultural Society. This was the beginning of the Wellington Botanic Garden. An adjacent 54 acres was granted in 1871, including a stand of native bush which was enormously valuable, as the original land had been cleared by settlers who needed timber and firewood. Sheltered gullies in the gardens today contain remnants of native forest that link back to the forest of pre-European settlement. The garden's oldest tree, a gnarled hinau in the Stable gully, is over 200 years old. The 10-hectare gardens offer something for everyone – amazing plant collections, duck pond, private picnicking and an adventure playground.

The *Treehouse*, the garden's education centre, was developed as a joint venture between Wellington City Council and WWF, the conservation organisation. There's an exhibition area, informaton desk and staff on hand. Opening times vary and admission is free.

The *Lady Norwood Rose Garden*, at the bottom of the hill, blooms spectacularly in colour and perfume from November to May. These gardens were created in 1953 and named after the wife of a former Wellington mayor. Formal beds showcase traditional rose varieties and recent hybrids, climbers and patio roses. The fountain in the centre is over 100 years old and originally graced the front of a London bank. Garden benches and lush grass make this an ideal place to rest and enjoy.

The *Begonia House* contains tropical and temperate displays featuring orchids, impatiens, begonias, coleus and large trees such as the huge-leafed King Fig. There's also a shop and a visitor information display. *Admission* free. *Open* daily in summer 10am– 5pm, and winter 10am–4pm. The *Garden Café* is open next door for light meals and ice cream, and alongside you'll see the *Peace Flame Garden* containing the preserved fires from the atomic holocaust at Hiroshima.

Linking the gardens to the city centre is the **Bolton Street Memorial Park**, the original settlers' cemetery that now straddles the motorway. The land was set aside for burials in 1840, and for the next 50 years was administered as three separate cemeteries – Church of England, Jewish and public. It served the town until 1892 when it was closed, except for new burials on existing plots. A 1967 act allowed the motorway to proceed, and burials then ceased. A large portion of the cemetery was taken for the motorway resulting in 3693 disinterments – these remains now rest in other parts of the cemetery. The cemetery is a peaceful island in time, with its old-fashioned roses and worn stones. The small chapel features stories and insights into the early Wellington settlement. To learn more, take the heritage trail, brochures for which are available in the chapel or at the upper and lower entrances to the park.

The gardens are also home to the **Carter Observatory**, New Zealand's national astronomy centre (see MUSEUMS), as well as an excellent adventure playground (for direct access, park on Glenmore Street and follow the signs up the hill).

OTARI–WILTON'S BUSH

160 Wilton Road, Wilton, tel 475-3245, www.wellington.govt.nz

Wellington's jewel. This is the only garden in New Zealand dedicated solely to native plants. It contains over 1200 species, native hybrids and cultivars from the sub-Antarctic islands in the south to Cape Reinga at the top of the North Island. Otari–Wilton's Bush plays an important part in native plant conservation, research and education, and offers its visitors a richly rewarding and pleasurable experience.

Otari–Wilton's Bush was originally covered with dense conifer broadleaf forest. Maori used the forest for hunting, hence the name Otari, which means 'place of snares'. Following European colonisation, some of the large trees were felled for timber and parts were burnt for farmland. One early landowner, Job Wilton, had the good foresight to preserve a piece of original forest and fence it off, hence the name Wilton's Bush. More remnant forest adjacent was protected after 1900, and in 1926 the Otari Open Air Native Plant Museum was established by Dr Leonard Cockayne and J. G. McKenzie. It's their vision of native plant conservation and education that you see in the gardens today.

So, what will you see at Otari? Ninety hectares of podocarps such as totara, rimu and matai, and around 150 species of flowering, perching and climbing plants such as native passionfruit, supplejack and rata. In the upper slopes, kohekohe, rewarewa, tawa and mahoe trees merge with forest remnants of old rimu and matai. Watch out for native birds such as tui, kereru, fantail, silver eye, kingfisher, grey warbler and morepork.

The information centre, *Te Marae O Tane*, is closest to the Wilton Road entrance (open daily 9am–5pm), and *guided tours* are available by donation (telephone in advance to book). The *canopy walkway* provides gorgeous green views, and is the start of an excellent *nature trail* (booklets from the information centre, 30–60 minutes). In all there are 11 km of *circular walks* to enjoy, all clearly signposted, weaving through forest and open grass area.

There are many places to rest and reflect, and plenty of picnic spots including the idyllic streamside *Troup Picnic Spot* with coin-operated barbecues. There's wheelchair access from the Wilton Road carpark to the information centre, the canopy walkway and the lookout. Dogs are welcome, on a lead, but must leave only footprints!

Otari is a short 5 km drive from the city centre, with car parks on Wilton Road and Wilton's Bush Road. Public transport is available via the frequent no. 14 bus from Lambton Quay. Note: there's no food for miles. *Open* every day from sunrise to sunset. *Admission* is free (but do look out for the koha/donation box).

FRANK KITTS PARK

Spectacularly located on the city waterfront, Frank Kitts Park was named after Wellington's longest serving mayor (1956–74) and is built on reclaimed land and an area that was once a wharf. There are various sculptures and plaques, an amphitheatre (used for summer concerts) and a playground with the best slide in town.

CENTRAL PARK

Brooklyn Road, Brooklyn

A large park with lots of paths, big trees and a stream to explore. The playground features a mixture of lots of new and old equipment set in a large open grassed space. Loads of swings, a flying fox, slides, see-saws, swingboat, etc. Good afternoon sun in winter.

BEN BURN PARK
Campbell Street, Karori

A large playing field and plenty of room for picnicking. The playground has a large wooden adventure-style structure, with slides, climbing frame, wobbly bridge and fireman's pole. There's a maze and swings alongside. A fenced-off area has safety matting and equipment for younger children.

KARORI PARK
400 Karori Road, Karori

An expanse of playing fields with cricket nets and skateboarding park alongside. The playground is attractive with safety matting throughout, nice new equipment and the bonus of a flying fox.

KHANDALLAH PARK
Woodmancote Road, Khandallah

This is a lovely bushy park with a play area with tracks leading off to Mt Kau Kau and the **Northern Walkway**. A large grassed area offers excellent picnicking and a shallow stream is good for paddling. The playground features a flying fox, slides, swings, and toddlers' climbing frame. The outdoor pool is open in summer (see page 68).

CARRARA PLAY AREA
Regent Street (off Owen Street), Newtown

Plenty of grass and a good wide bike path. Lots of equipment such as tunnels, car, swing-bridge, swinging bars, tyre and flying fox. Safety matting.

KILBIRNIE PARK
Corner Kilbirnie Crescent & Evans Bay Parade, Kilbirnie

A great playground beside the library with slide, bridge and swings. Smaller adventure playground, enclosed with gate to keep toddlers in. See-saw, ramps, tunnels, steps and slide. Sports field nearby.

SHORLAND PARK
Reef Street, Island Bay

A lovely seaside playground with a range of equipment including swings. Plenty of room for picnicking.

CHURCHILL PARK
2 Marine Parade, Seatoun
A beachside playground with good equipment set within a huge grassed area with lots of space to run around. Plenty of adventure by the seaside.

GRASSLEES RESERVE
Luckie Street, Tawa
A very pleasant streamside park with ducks to feed. There's a modern adventure playground with safety matting, see-saws and swings, plus a large concrete arena for skating. Good picnicking spots.

BISHOP PARK
Marine Parade, Eastbourne
Home of the north island's longest slide, plus loads of other great equipment including swings and a flying fox. Special area for the under fives. Waterfront location; fantastic for family picnics. Swimming pool next door, and shops close by.

HAEWAI WIND GARDENS AND MEADERY
236 Houghton Bay Road, Houghton Bay, tel 387-9541, www.windgardens.com
You can find Jacob and Carol's rustic Wind Gardens just 10 minutes drive from the centre of Wellington, barely fifty metres from the dramatic south coast at Houghton Bay. This is a harsh climate, with the garden blasted frequently by north and salt-laden south winds. The beauty of the garden is its diversity and relaxed feel. Perennials and shrubs, natives, exotics and cottage garden plants have been orchestrated together, evolving and thriving with the elements. Nestled in the garden is the *Meadery*, housed in an 1865 settlers cottage. The organic mead brewed here is carefully crafted from honey, yeast and spring water (from a natural spring on site) and is delicious and a tonic to boot – tastings and purchases on offer. *Admission* and mead tastings $5. *Open* daily for mead tastings Mon–Fri 12.30pm–7.30pm, Sat/Sun 11am–6pm; bookings recommended.

Wildlife

KARORI WILDLIFE SANCTUARY

Tour bookings tel 920-9200, info line 920-2222, www.sanctuary.org.nz
The Karori Wildlife Sanctuary is the world's first inner-city predator-free environment. Internationally recognised as a unique community conservation project, the sanctuary provides a safe haven for New Zealand's treasured endangered wildlife. It is a place where you can step back in time, experience a slice of New Zealand's natural heritage and enjoy the peaceful scenic surroundings.

A 2.3 metre-high predator-proof fence surrounds the 252-hectare valley. Introduced pests and predators have been removed from the valley and rare native wildlife such as the little spotted kiwi, the North Island robin, weka, bellbird, whitehead, brown teal, North Island saddleback and North Island kaka have been released. A carefully planned conservation and restoration programme ensures that native flora and fauna are progressively introduced. The knowledge and experience developed here will have far reaching applications in contributing to world conservation.

The sanctuary is situated around two old reservoirs that in earlier days supplied Wellington's rapidly growing city with water and now support a newly created wetland environment. The deep valley, formed by the *Wellington Fault* (see WELCOME), was also the

Karori Wildlife Sanctuary

scene of an unfruitful gold rush in 1869. Small claim tunnels still exist in the area and one of the claim tunnels, the Morning Star, has been restored. Visitors can walk into the tunnel and also look down into the shaft from a viewing area above. Historic buildings in the heritage area exhibit informative displays of the valley's past. There are also a wide range of walking tracks, picnic spots and activity sites suitable for everyone.

You can walk round the sanctuary at your leisure during normal open hours or book a customised guided tour during the day or night. On a nocturnal tour you can hear the call of native nocturnal species like morepork, weka and New Zealand's most precious bird – the kiwi. Experienced guides take you along a well-developed trail where you pass two reservoirs, historical buildings, a 'shag roost' tree and also see wonderful displays of New Zealand glow-worms.

The sanctuary's book, *Developing A Sanctuary*, explains all about the project and the 500-year plan to restore the valley. It's available for sale alongside other books, clothing, small toys and other souvenirs in the visitor centre.

Admission adult $6, child (school age) $3, family (2 adults/3 children) $15, please ask for tour prices (all profits go back to the sanctuary). The visitor centre is located at the end of Waiapu Road (first left after the Karori Tunnel). Car parking is available. *Open* daily (Dec–Mar) 10am–5pm; (April–Nov) Mon–Fri 10am–4pm, Sat/Sun 10am–5pm. Closed Christmas Day.

To learn more about the conservation and protection of wildlife and wild places, visit the website of *Forest and Bird* (www.forestandbird.org.nz), New Zealand's leading independent conservation organisation. Their *Kiwi Conservation Club* (www.kcc.org.nz) is especially for children.

SEAL COAST SAFARI

55 Hobart Street, Miramar, tel 025-534-880/0800-SEAL-2R, www.sealcoast.com
Explore the dramatic coastline and rugged remoteness of the 'Seal Coast' stretching west from Owhiro Bay Quarry to Tongue Point and the Leaning Lighthouse on Wellington's south coast. Your four-wheel drive journey takes you to visit the seals via a hill country station that takes in the local high point (Hawkins Hill, 500 m), and the lowest (the Wellington faultline which dips down to sea level at Long Bay). Expect seals all year round (money back guarantee!). Your professional guide has extensive knowledge of the region. *Cost* adult $59, and $10 for up to two accompanying children (other children half price). *Tours* take just under 3 hours, and run twice daily departing *Wellington Visitor Centre* at 10.30am and 1.30pm.

WELLINGTON ZOO

200 Daniell Street, Newtown, tel 381-6750, www.wellingtonzoo.com

The oldest zoo in New Zealand, Wellington Zoo was founded in April 1906 when the Bostok & Wombwell Circus presented a young lion to Wellington. The lion was initially housed at the Botanic Garden along with a small collection of animals, but in 1907 part of Newtown Park was allocated as their new home. The zoo grew rapidly, and by 1912 around 500 animals were housed in cages, aviaries and a huge sea lion pool. The Wellington Zoological Society was largely responsible for the early growth and development of the zoo through its donations of large numbers of animals and plants. World War II slowed down the zoo's development until the 1950s, when the zoo's role was to entertain the public with elephant rides, performing goats and chimpanzee tea parties.

In line with changing attitudes, modern zoos around the world now provide more natural environments for their animals. At Wellington Zoo, the tiger, monkey, lion, chimpanzee and baboon enclosures have been extensively redeveloped over the past 20 years. On the *Tropical River Trail* visitors are surrounded by a rainforest habitat, separated only by a moat from three species of primates.

Wellington Zoo is committed to a future in conservation and education. It is actively involved in international captive breeding programmes for both native and exotic endangered species. The aim is to maintain sufficient genetic diversity to sustain viable breeding populations. Equally important is the zoo's role in raising visitors' awareness of the importance of conservation.

Scheduled *keeper talks* are held every day including the pelican feed, tigers, chimps, giraffes and baboons, and other talks are held on different days.

Bring a picnic for lunch, or visit the food services on site. *Zoolittles* shop stocks animal-themed gifts and products for all ages including puppets, posters and ostrich eggs (yes, that's right!).

Free parking; pushchair hire; free wheelchair use; Zoo Cruiser for those with mobility problems. *Admission* adult $9, child (3–16) $4, under 3s free; family concessions $17–26; annual passes also available. *Open* daily 9.30am–5pm; open late in summer.

ISLAND BAY MARINE EDUCATION CENTRE

396 The Esplanade, Island Bay, tel 383-8285, www.islandbay.wellington.net.nz
Learn about the marine life of Wellington's unique rocky shore.
Open the first weekend of each month, the centre has a large
variety of live habitat displays and a chance to get up close to
plants and animals. The centre's aim is to 'foster respect and
appreciation for local marine life and explore the role humans play
in this and other habitats'. *Admission* by donation. *Open* first full
weekend of every month only, entry is at 10am, 12pm and 2pm or by
arrangement.

STAGLANDS WILDLIFE RESERVE

Akatarawa Road, Upper Hutt, tel 526-7529, www.staglands.co.nz
Set amongst the beautiful bush of the scenic Akatarawa Valley,
Staglands offers a heart-warming encounter with nature. Set in 10
hectares of what was formerly paddocks, the aim of founder John
Simister was to create a balanced eco-system. Over 30 years, the
land has been replanted, attracting many native birds and insects
who share their home with pigs, horses, donkeys, guinea pigs,
goats, deer and trout. Touch and hand-feed the wildlife, or go on a
pony ride. A play area, barbecue facilities and café help makes this
a wonderful day out for the whole family. *Admission* adult $10, child
$5. *Open* daily 10am–5pm.

NGA MANU NATURE RESERVE

Ngarara Road, Waikanae, tel (04) 293-4131, www.ngamanu.co.nz
This 15-hectare reserve contains the largest remnant of original
lowland swamp forest on the Kapiti Coast, and here you can see
a diverse range of native flora and fauna including many on the
threatened species list. You'll see some of over 56 different bird
species such as kiwi, morepork, tui, wood pigeon, fantail, scaup,
blue duck, kakariki, teal and paradise duck along with tuatara,
gecko, skinks and wetas. Feed the eels daily at 2pm, or visit the
nocturnal house. It'll take about an hour to drive from Wellington
City. *Admission* adult $7.50, child (under 15) $3.50, family $15. *Open*
daily 10am–5pm.

KAPITI ISLAND

Situated about 5 km off the west coast, Kapiti Island is an internationally important reserve, home to some of the world's most endangered birds. The island is totally free of all introduced predators, the wildlife flourishing as a result. A 90-minute walk with plenty of opportunities for bird watching takes you up to the 520-metre summit with magnificent 360° views. The island is rich in Maori and whaling history, and there's great swimming and snorkelling in the *Kapiti Marine Reserve*. There are two options for visiting the island.

Self-guided excursions are possible by obtaining a landing permit from the Department of Conservation (cost adult $9, child $4.50). Two transport operators offer services departing from Paraparaumu Beach in front of the Kapiti Boating Club:

Kapiti Marine Charter (tel 800-433-779, www.kapitimarinecharter.co.nz)
Kapiti Tours (tel 0800-527-484, www.kapititours.co.nz).

In addition, *Kapiti Alive* (www.kapitiislandalive.co.nz, tel 027-288-3771) offers overnight home stay and tours of the northern end of the island (numberes are limited, so book well in advance).

For more information including permit and tour options, contact *DOC Visitor Information Centre* (Government Buildings, Lambton Quay, tel 472-7356, www.doc.govt.nz).

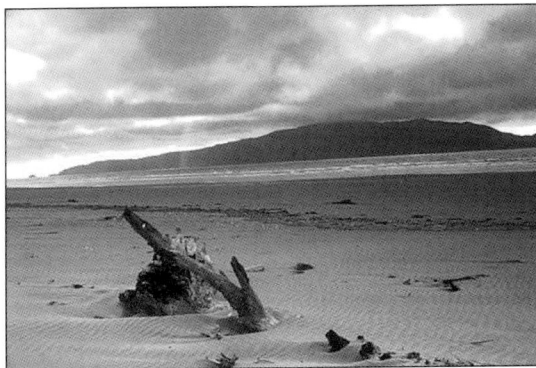

Peter Sundstrom

MOUNT BRUCE NATIONAL WILDLIFE CENTRE

SH2, tel (06) 375-8004, www.mtbruce.doc.govt

Set in 1000 hectares of lush rainforest, Mt Bruce is DOC's national centre for the captive management of endangered birds. Established 'for the protection of New Zealand's wildlife and habitats', this award-winning wildlife centre is managed by the Department of Conservation in partnership with the National Wildlife Centre Trust and Rangitaane o Wairarapa. One of the key roles of Mt Bruce is to raise awareness, educate and inform people about conservation in New Zealand. Here you get an opportunity to meet experienced conservation staff at work.

The 'captive management team' are responsible for managing breeding programmes for some of New Zealand's most endangered birds, including kokako, hihi (stitchbird) and shore plover, amongst others. Some of these birds are released on to offshore islands, and some released into the Mt Bruce/Pukaha forest itself, where it is hoped they will breed.

The feeding of eels (1.30pm) and kaka (3pm) provide a good opportunity to get a bit closer, and excellent interpretive bush walks take you through lowland podocarp forest. Visit the *Kiwi Nocturnal House*, view displays and video presentations and enjoy espresso and light meals in *Café Takahe*.

The Mt Bruce centre is approximately 30 minutes north of Masterton, about 2 hours drive from Wellington city. *Admission* adult $8, child (under 17) free. *Open* daily 9am–4.30pm.

Mount Bruce National Wildlife Centre

City Walks

Wellington is renowned for its compact size and the best way to explore it is on foot. There are plenty of **heritage trails** that tell you more about the city, and some wonderful **walkways**, many with magnificent views.

The *Wellington City Council* produces maps and guides for the walks below, available from the *Visitor Information Centre* and other visitor thoroughfares. Please note, though: some trail maps are under revision and not readily available.

HERITAGE TRAILS

Explore the city's nooks and crannies on these trails, most of which will take around 2–4 hours.

Te Aro Explore the character of Cuba Street as you wander its narrow streets. Look into the changing face of the city from the 1840s to the present.

Maritime Wellington An amble along the waterfront. Highlights include the **Wellington Museum of City and Sea**, historic wharf buildings and **Te Papa**. Wheelchair friendly.

The Old Shoreline A journey of imagination along the old shoreline, before reclamation took place. One hundred and fifty years of history, from the settlement's infancy to today's modern city.

Art Deco in the Capital A join-the-dots trail of 30 art deco buildings – all characterised by their geometrical decoration and imposing grandeur.

Aro Valley – Cottages, Crannies and Curiosities Explore the historic Aro Valley and around. Highlights include the **Colonial Cottage Museum** and the largest collection of unaltered colonial working class houses in Wellington.

Thorndon – Power, Passion, Prose and Piety Thorndon is New Zealand's oldest suburb, and rich in history. Highlights include **Old Saint Paul's, Katherine Mansfield's birthplace** and the Tinakori lanes.

Te Ara o Nga Tupuna — The Path of Our Ancestors A combination driving/walking trail of the eastern and southern suburbs. Visit Maori historic sites including pa (fortified place), marae (meeting ground) and kainga (place of residence).

Karori A longer trail through New Zealand's largest and Wellington's first suburb, best covered with transport. Visit an historic tunnel, cemetery, chapel and fortress.

Northern Suburbs A walking and driving tour of Wellington's northern suburbs including Wadestown, Johnsonville and Ohariu. Explore historic Maori sites and the Ngaio railway settlement.

Petone Discover the the story of the original Wellington settlement, from its start as dense forest and swamp, to the pa of chief Te Puni, early British settlement, to today.

OTHER ART AND HERITAGE WALKS

Waterfront from Post Office Square to Te Papa (EXPLORE WELLINGTON WALK 1) A stroll along the waterfront. Highlights include Queens Wharf with its historic offices and storehouses. View sculpture in **Frank Kitts Park** and **Civic Square**.

Courtenay Place to Cuba Street (EXPLORE WELLINGTON WALK 2) Walk through Courtenay Place and Cuba Street with their many old buildings, murals and the famous **bucket fountain**.

Business District (EXPLORE WELLINGTON WALK 3) Explore the business end of town via Willis Street, Lambton Quay and Featherston Street. Varied architecture and modern sculpture, with retail therapy en route.

Railway Station to Thorndon (EXPLORE WELLINGTON WALK 4) Discover the early history of the Wellington settlement. Lots of landmark buildings and sculpture.

Bolton Street Memorial Trail This stroll through the original Wellington cemetery with its worn headstones and old roses allows a fascinating insight into the lives of early Wellingtonians.

Walkways

The following walkway routes are all clearly marked, but interpretative maps available from the *Wellington Visitor Centre* will enhance your enjoyment. Unless you have a car or bicycle (or good legs), you'll need a public transport connection to/from the track end. This is as easy as calling *Ridewell* on 801-7000, or finding a friend with wheels. There are loads of shortcuts on all these routes if you don't want to walk the whole way. Dogs may come with you, on a lead.

CITY TO SEA WALKWAY
4 hours, 12 km, City (Parliament) to Island Bay
A good way to get to know Wellington. On the way you'll pass through the **Botanic Garden**, two historic cemeteries and several observatories, see turn of the century cottages, and walk along the town belt, coming out at the rocky shore of Island Bay.

SOUTHERN WALKWAY
4–5 hours, 11 km, Oriental Bay to Houghton Bay/Island Bay
The greatest attraction of this walkway is variety: from views of the harbour and central city at **Oriental Bay**, to the shade and tranquillity of the town belt forest, to the exposed south coast. Steep in places but not difficult overall.

NORTHERN WALKWAY
4 hours, 16 km, Kelburn to Johnsonville
This walkway has many attractions including spectacular views, picnic sites and playgrounds, disused tunnels and the serenity of the bush. On the way you pass the **Botanic Garden**, **Tinakori Hill** and **Khandallah Park**. Easy to cut short or complete in stages.

SKYLINE WALKWAY
2 hours, 4 km, Chartwell to Mt Kau Kau (Khandallah)
The great thing about this walk is that you follow an undulating ridge with non-stop panoramic views. On a clear day you'll see the Kaikoura Ranges, the Marlborough Sounds, the city and harbour, and the Tararua and Orongorongo Ranges. See CITY LOOKOUTS for another **Mt Kau Kau** route.

EASTERN WALKWAY

1.5 hours, 2.5 km, Pass of Branda (Seatoun) to Tarakena Bay
A fascinating walk along southern end of the Miramar Peninsula offering spectacular views of the craggy south coast, Pencarrow Head and out to sea. Lots of expansive views and fresh sea air.

The Wahine Disaster

On the stormy morning of April 1968, the inter-island ferry *Wahine* with 734 people aboard struck Barrett Reef, suffering severe hull damage and losing the use of both engines. Anchors where dropped but these were dragged as *Wahine* was blown toward Point Dorset. At 1.20pm, as she listed to starboard, passengers were ordered to abandon ship. Shortly after 2pm off Steeple Rock where she was first struck, Wahine sank to the seabed, resting on her starboard side.

That day, many acts of heroism and valour were performed in the attempts to rescue and bring ashore the survivors. Most passengers were washed ashore on the rugged east coast of the harbour, but 51 people lost their lives. The *Wellington Museum of City and Sea* houses a permanent display of this event; particularly moving is the beautiful short film by Gaylene Preston.

Walk Wellington (tel 384-9590) offers tours for walkers of all ages. The *Essential Wellington* walk leaves daily from Nov–Mar: 10am Wed/Fri/ Sat/Sun, and 5.30pm Mon/Tues/Thurs; April–Oct: 10am Sat/Sun only (adult $20, child $10). *Speciality walks* (including art, heritage, nature and shopping) and personalised tours can also be arranged. Book at the *Wellington Visitor Centre* (tel 802-4860).

On Sundays, *Te Aro heritage walks* are guided by **Campaign for a Better City** (www.cbc.org.nz). Meet at 1pm at the junction of Cuba Street and Tonks Avenue, opposite Arthur Street; *koha* (donation) appreciated.

FOR MORE INFORMATION ...

Feeling Great www.feelinggreat.co.nz

Walking Wellington by Kathy Ombler, an easy to read walking guidebook, available from bookshops.

Scenic Reserves, Regional and Forest Parks

Wellington offers the best of both worlds, because when it's time to take a break from city hubbub, you don't have to go too far for more natural pleasures. This region is packed with scenic reserves, and regional and forest parks, so there's something for everyone in the great outdoors. Green is the theme, and it's good for the soul.

Popular parks and reserves are listed here, divided into **City Central**, **City–Kapiti** and **City–Wairarapa**. All are managed by either the *Department of Conservation* or *Greater Wellington Regional Council* (as indicated). We recommend you check with them if you have questions about bikes, dogs, and hut and camping passes. Hunting permits and fishing licences are required, so ask about these too.

Generally, *Regional Parks* are open from sunrise to sunset, and *Scenic Reserves & Forest Parks* all the time. Entry is free, although you will have to pay for hut passes and camping.

Department of Conservation (DOC) www.doc.govt.nz
Government Buildings, Lambton Quay
(opposite the Beehive), tel 472-7356

Greater Wellington Regional Council (GW) www.doc.govt.nz
142 Wakefield Street, tel 384-5708; or
1056 Fergusson Drive, Upper Hutt, tel 526-4133,

City Central

TE KOPAHOU RESERVE

A variety of walking (and mountain biking) tracks can be found in this important 600-hectare conservation reserve with its dramatic views of the Cook Strait. It's popular for walking, beachcombing and hopping around the rock pools, and also for diving, surfcasting and seal spotting. The **Red Rocks Coastal Walk** (2–3 hours) takes you from the Owhiro Bay carpark along the rocky shore to the seal 'haul out' (seals May–Oct). If you don't want to walk, it's a great bike ride, and tours also operate around here (see WILDLIFE). Vehicle access is via Owhiro Bay Parade (seaside) or Ashton Fitchett Drive, Brooklyn (hillside). **DOC**

Lindsay Keats

MATIU/SOMES ISLAND

Lying in the harbour 8 km from the city centre, Matiu/Somes is one of New Zealand's most accessible predator-free islands. This prominent landmark was until recently off-limits to the general public, but in 1995 passed into the care of the Department of Conservation. It's a regionally significant breeding site for several threatened bird species and one of the few places to see tuatara in the wild (the last surviving representative of reptiles which appeared on Earth 200 million years ago, at the same time as the dinosaurs). The Cook Strait giant weta also lives there.

According to Maori oral history, the legendary Maori explorer Kupe named the island and its tiny neighbour Matiu and Makoro after his nieces when he sailed into the harbour 1000 years ago. The islands were renamed Somes and Ward islands by the New Zealand Company in 1839. In 1997 the island was renamed Matiu/Somes.

From the 1870s, Somes Island was a quarantine station for animals and humans (until the 1920s travellers suspected of carrying diseases such as smallpox were quarantined there, and war internees detained there during both world wars). Shortly after World War II, the local branch of the Royal Forest and Bird Protection Society began habitat restoration and established a nursery. When rats were eradicated in 1987, the island's conservation value was greatly enhanced and the quarantine station closed for good.

A visit to Matiu/Somes is a wonderful outing with its interesting history, natural beauty and unique 360° panorama. There's no fee to land on the island, so you just need to pay for the **Dominion Post Ferry** (see TRAVEL AND TRANSPORT). Ring the ferry office for details (the island is sometimes closed due to fire danger, Jan–Mar). **DOC**

From Makara

This time it isn't cloud
whisked up, set into landscape
the kind that might trick
an inexperienced sailor

into sighting a fabulous coast.
Today the air is playing it
straight; and that is the white
of the South decorating the sky.

Some try to swim over;
or there's the quick route
along the cliff, winding up
through hebe and gorse

on a track that clutches so hard
it's worn to a groove
(the sea below laying out its net
of green and purple): to where

the batteries used to swing
from horizon to horizon.
Suddenly, the South sets out
to meet you, breaking

off into islands that strain
to become buoyant; opening up
its channels like the space
between arms to you:
                                        Jump,

is the advice, launch yourself
into the gap; and something
will reach out far enough
to gather you across.

BILL SEWELL

Makara is a salt-crusted corner of Wellington that will amaze you with its wind-blasted beauty, angry surf, and freaky flotsam and jetsam.

Makara's high cliffs have for centuries provided tangata whenua good vantage points for defence, and a pa site lies on the western promontory of Fisherman's Bay. Cliff-top gun emplacements mark the position of Fort Opau, a World War II garrison.

There's a loop walk (2–3 hours) and, although the inland section is closed for lambing 1 August–31 October, a splendid walk can still be had along the beach or up to the gun emplacements, where you'll get expansive views of the Cook Strait, Tasman Sea, Kaikoura Ranges, and Mana and Kapiti Islands. The coastal section requires scrambling over boulders and loose rocks, so sturdy footwear is recommended. Makara is sheltered from southerly winds, but the northerly can blow pretty hard – fun for the adults, but a bit scary for the featherweights There's a beachside café with ice cream and snacks.

Makara is accessible from Karori (follow the signs from the end of Karori Road) or Johnsonville through the picturesque *Ohariu Valley* with its rural attractions. *DOC*

EAST HARBOUR REGIONAL PARK

Situated between Eastbourne and Wainuiomata, this is a landscape of bush-clad hills, sheltered valleys, freshwater wetlands, rocky headlands and sweeping bays. The park's highlight is the **Pencarrow Coastal Trail** that starts at the end of Murutai Road in Eastbourne, sidling along the coast to historic *Pencarrow Lighthouse* and the twin lakes *Kohangapiripiri* and *Kohangatera* with their abundant bird life. Further on lie the remains of the *Paiaka*, wrecked in 1906, and dramatic *Baring Head* with its cliffs and beach boulders. The track is flat and easy for folk of all ages and fitness levels, and the views are spectacular. It's 8 km to the lighthouse – that'll take you a couple of hours on foot, but it makes a much better bike ride. Bike hire is available at the track start. To protect native wildlife, dogs are not permitted.

Pencarrow's Lady of the Lamp

In 1859, the country's first permanent lighthouse was built at Pencarrow, and New Zealand's first paid lighthouse keeper was appointed: Mary Jane Bennett. More than 140 years later Mary holds the distinction of being New Zealand's only woman lighthouse keeper, an honour she's unlikely to lose as all New Zealand's 23 lighthouses are now automated.

From Eastbourne's **Days Bay**, you can access the *Eastern Bays* and *Butterfly Creek* tracks. There are four tracks to Butterfly Creek, with Kowhai Street the most popular (others are Mackenzie Road, Muritai Park, Bus Barn). It will take you 2–4 hours return trip from any of the access roads. The tracks climb steeply through mixed regenerating bush into beech forest, and as you descend into the creek you pass some of the largest kahikatea in the park. A picnic area and toilet are provided near the junction of Butterfly Creek and Gollans Stream. There are various other loop tracks on the Eastern Bays, which also connect to the *Main Ridge Track*. This leads north to the *Wainuiomata Hill Road* summit, and is also met by the popular *Lees Grove Track*, which passes through some superb native bush and climbs to the highest point in the park, *Lowry Trig* (373 m). **GW**

City–Kapiti

COLONIAL KNOB SCENIC RESERVE

This reserve contains the most significant native forest remnant in the Tawa–Porirua basin. There are many short walks, and the 3–4 hour *Colonial Knob track* rises to 468 m with views possible from the Kaikoura Ranges in the south to Mt Taranaki in the northwest. Access is via Broken Hill Road, off Raiha Street, which connects Kenepuru Drive and Prosser Street in Elsdon, Porirua. *DOC*

BATTLE HILL FARM FOREST PARK

A long-established working farm and historic site of the 1846 battle between colonial forces and local Maori, Battle Hill offers pleasant horse-riding trails, easy walks through scenic bush and farmland, camping, picnicking and mountain biking. Dogs not permitted. Enter via the Paekakariki Hill Road 6 km north of Pauatahanui just off SH58. Park Ranger tel 237-5511. *GW*

QUEEN ELIZABETH PARK

This large coastal park is one of the last relatively unchanged areas of dune and wetland in Kapiti, and is deservedly popular for all-day family outings in the summer. It offers plenty of water sport opportunities (lifeguards patrol Paekakariki Beach in summer), a motor camp, horse-riding trails, picnicking and lots of room for running around. The beach is long, wide and sandy, and the sunsets quite spectacular (but don't let the gates close on you!). The **Wellington Tramway Museum** lies at the Mackay's Crossing entrance, offering 2 km rides to the beach during weekends and public holidays, plus interesting interpretative displays. Access is via Wellington Road, Paekakariki, Mackay's Crossing or The Esplanade in Raumati South, all off SH1. Park Ranger tel 292-8625. *GW*

HEMI MATENGA MEMORIAL PARK

This 330-hectare native forest overlooking Waikanae contains one of the largest remaining areas of kohekohe forest. The reserve rises steeply from 150 m to its highest point, Te Au (514 m), but there are walking tracks for people of all ages. Access is off Reikorangi Road, Waikanae. *DOC*

TARARUA FOREST PARK

This rugged landscape has a mountainous core of towering peaks, the highest of which is *Mt Mitre* (1571 m). Visible from Wellington city is the slightly shorter *Mt Hector* (1529 m). Extending from the Manawatu Gorge in the north to the Rimutaka Saddle in the south, Tararua Forest Park was the first to be established by the former New Zealand Forest Service in 1954, primarily for forest, water and soil conservation and public recreation. The 120,000-hectare park offers something for everyone – short walks through to multiple-day tramps, and can be accessed from both the west and east.

Otaki Forks is the main western entrance to the park. Two tributaries, the *Waiotauru River* and *Waitatapia Stream*, meet the *Otaki River* here. Open river terraces, pioneer stone walls and old boilers reflect the area's farming and sawmilling history. Active people will enjoy walks of all lengths and swimming in the river. There are basic facilities including a campground. Access via Otaki Gorge Road off SH1, 1.5 km south of Otaki. *DOC*

NEW ZEALAND

ENVIRONMENTAL
CARE CODE

Protect plants and animals
Remove rubbish
Bury toilet waste
Keep streams and lakes clean
Take care with fires
Camp carefully
Keep to the track
Consider others
Respect our cultural heritage
Enjoy your visit
Toitu te whenua (leave the land undisturbed)

Safety in the Outdoors

Be prepared for all weathers. If walking, wear strong shoes or boots and carry a waterproof jacket at all times. Take drinking water and high-energy food. Read the information boards at track entrances and obey all signs. Let someone know your intended route and return time, and allow plenty of time to return in daylight.

FOR MORE INFORMATION ...

Wellington Tramping & Mountaineering Club
www.wtmc.org.nz

Tararua Tramping Club
www.ttc.org.nz

City—Wairarapa

BELMONT REGIONAL PARK

Rolling farmland and bush-clad valleys provide an ideal place for picnics, horse riding, cross country running and mountain biking, short walks or longer tramps. The walks to the historic **Korokoro Dam**, **Belmont Trig** (457 m) and World War II munitions magazines are highlights. Open hilltops offer panoramic views and access to the eroded slopes of Boulder Hill. Dogs permitted only in Korokoro Valley. Access is via Cornish Street (Petone), Oakleigh Street, Stratton Street or Hill Road (Lower Hutt), Dry Creek (SH2/SH58 intersection), Takapu Road or Cannons Creek (Porirua). Park Ranger tel 586-6614. *GW*

AKATARAWA FOREST

Between Upper Hutt and Paraparaumu lies the 15,000-hectare Akatarawa Forest. This forest was extensively logged during the early twentieth century, and the old logging roads provide access for walking, horse riding, picnicking, trail bike riding, hunting, fishing and nature study. There is plenty of pine, but also regenerating native bush to explore. A warning though: most of the forest is rugged and isolated. You should keep to the marked tracks and take *Topographic Map R26* with you. Tramp with an experienced group. Access is via **Battle Hill Farm Forest Park**, Maungakotukutuku Road (SH1, 1 km north of MacKays Crossing), Karapoti Road (SH2, 3 km north of Upper Hutt and follow Akatarawa Road for 4 km) or Cooks Road (SH58 via Moonshine Road to Bulls Run Road then left to Cooks Road). Forest Ranger tel 025-248-1658. *GW*

HUTT RIVER TRAIL

This 24 km trail follows the Hutt River from Birchville through the Hutt Valley until it meets the sea in Petone. It offers easy and scenic cycling and walking as well as river access for swimming, fishing and canoeing. In many areas there are tracks on both sides of river, allowing various routes and loops. Convenient entry and cross-over points are the bridges at the Hutt Estuary, Ava, Ewen, Melling, Kennedy Good, Silverstream, Moonshine, Totara Park, Harcourt Park and Birchville. Public transport access is readily available (*Ridewell*, tel 801-7000). Park Ranger tel 027-283-7991. *GW*

KAITOKE REGIONAL PARK

The steep, bush-clad Kaitoke hills enclose excellent sheltered picnic and camping facilities. Take a short bush walk, or enjoy swimming and other watery activities on the *Hutt River*. The 3-hour *Ridge Track* links the Pakuratahi and Te Marua ends of the park and offers splendid views of the Hutt Valley. Note that the Hutt Gorge river trip takes 3–6 hours and can be dangerous. Wear a wetsuit, lifejacket and helmet and inform the ranger of your intentions. Access is via Kaitoke Waterworks Road off SH2, 15 km north of Upper Hutt, or Te Marua, 6 km north of Upper Hutt. Park Ranger tel 526-7322. **GW**

RIMUTAKA FOREST PARK

Just 45 minutes drive from downtown Wellington, **Catchpool Valley** is the most popular entrance to the 22,000-hectare Rimutaka Forest Park. Within the valley are lovely short walks and day trips, a campground and picnic/barbecue facilities. It takes about 2 hours to walk from the car park into the river valley, an amazing hidden wonderland. This is a very good tramp for children. A visitor centre has displays, a small shop and 24-hour telephone. DOC-managed cabins in the Orongorongo River valley are available for hire, booked well in advance. Access is via Wainuiomata – follow the Coast Road for 12 km. The gates close at dusk and reopen at 8am.

A further 10 km down the Coast Road from the Catchpool gate is the **Turakirae Head Scientific Reserve**, so named for the headland (rae) where the Rimutaka Ranges come down (turakae) to the sea. This is a valuable habitat for a variety of plants and wildlife including hundreds of fur seals, which are at their highest numbers during winter. (Never approach seals too closely, and do not get between a seal and the sea.) The walk from the car park to the Head takes about 45 minutes, and it's another hour to the eastern edge of the reserve. The coast is popular for surfcasting, diving and (brave) surfing. **DOC**

TUNNEL GULLY RECREATION AREA

Tunnel Gully is nestled at the foot of *Mt Climie* (830 m) north of Upper Hutt. Eighteen hectares have been developed for picnics, mountain biking and walking. Toilets are provided, and the shallow water of Collins Stream is ideal for paddling and swimming for young children. There are a number of interesting and challenging walks to enjoy including *Tane's Track* (1-hour loop) and the *Mt Climie summit* (allow 3 hours return). Access is via Plateau Road, Te Marua, 7.5 km north of Upper Hutt on SH2. Forest Ranger tel 025-248-1658. *GW*

RIMUTAKA RAIL TRAIL

Set in the native and exotic forests of the *Rimutaka Ranges* north of Upper Hutt, this track leads you toward and along the former Wellington–Wairarapa rail route. This easy-graded 18 km track passes through historic (spooky!) tunnels and over picturesque bridges, while interpretative displays tell the story of the railway. The trail offers walking, mountain biking for riders of all levels, swimming, fishing, picnicking and camping, and connects, as it should, with the Wairarapa. Access is off SH2 near the start of the Rimutaka Hill. Forest Ranger tel 025-248-1658. *GW* (Upper Hutt access); *DOC* (Wairarapa access).

The Wairarapa side of the **TARARUA FOREST PARK** can be accessed via the popular *Holdsworth* camping ground and picnic area. Set against the backdrop of some of the highest peaks in the Tararua Range, Holdsworth offers short walks and longer tramps through attractive forest vegetation and higher up into the alpine environment. The picturesque *Atiwhakatu Stream* is good for swimming, and home to all sorts of bird and insect life. There's a ranger on site, and secluded camping, lodge, barbecue and picnic facilities. There's red deer, wild goats and pigs, brown trout and eel. Access is off Norfolk Road, 2 km south of Masterton on SH2. *DOC*

   Another eastern entrance to the Tararuas is via *Waiohine Gorge*, a popular camping and recreation area. The gorge is spectacular, good for swimming, rafting, tubing and kayaking. Access is via Dalefield Road, 2 km south of Carterton on SH2.

   Not far from here is the *Carter Scenic Reserve*, a pretty patchwork landscape of swamp and semi-swamp forest on two old terraces of the *Ruamahanga River*. What you see here was once typical of the Wairarapa – grass, wetland, shrubland and forest. There are many short walks and trout fishing. Access is via Gladstone Road, 12 km southeast of Carterton. **DOC**

AORANGI FOREST PARK

This 19,373-hectare park lies between *Martinborough* and *Cape Palliser*. For access, follow the Martinborough–Pirinoa Road for about 50 minutes to the Cape Palliser road turn-off. It's a further 37 km to Cape Palliser (some unsealed surfaces), and the roadside attractions and dramatic scenery make this a classic seaside drive. The coast is popular for surfcasting, diving and surfing, but note: it is not safe for swimming. **DOC**

A main attraction along the road is the **Putangirua Pinnacles Scenic Reserve** with its campsite and short walks with open sea views. When the Aorangi Range was an island, 7–9 million years ago, screes poured gravels on to the coast, much as they do today around Cape Palliser. The *Putangirua Stream* has exposed this ancient layer to erosion from rain and flood and, to cut a long story short, that's how these spectacular pinnacles or 'hoodoos' are formed. There are three walking routes to the Pinnacles from the car park; allow 2–3 hours for the round trip. The car park is about 13 km from the Lake Ferry turn-off, about an hour's drive from Martinborough.

The road continues to the tiny fishing village of **Ngawi** with its gallery of fishing boats and beachside tractors. Continuing onward from here you'll reach dramatic **Cape Palliser**. The lighthouse dates back to 1897, and the view at the top is well worth the 250 steps. There's a fur seal colony too. This is a fascinating corner of the region, rich in history, offering a glimpse into the life of a remote and rugged fishing village.

Those looking for something even further afield might like to visit the jaw-droppingly dramatic **Castlepoint Scenic Reserve** (birds, beach, reef, lagoon, lighthouse, cliffs, seals, dolphins and daisies). Access is via Masterton, and it will take about 3 hours to get there from downtown Wellington. **DOC**

Mountain Biking

Wellington is not the place for a bicycle with one gear. You really need 18 or 27, and that's why mountain bikes are so popular here. This city is fantastic for off-road cyclists of every age and ability – there are heaps of good tracks already, and more are planned.

A special thank you to the Kennett Brothers, who supplied the following content from their excellent *Classic New Zealand Mountain Bike Rides* (Kennett Bros & P. Morgan, from bookshops).

MAKARA PEAK MOUNTAIN BIKE PARK

South Karori Road, www.makarapeak.org.nz, bike hire from Mud Cycles
The Makara Peak park has justifiably caught the attention of mountain bikers worldwide, with descriptions such as 'epic' and 'legendary' featuring amongst its praises. Only 8 km from the city, this bushy park offers tracks for riders of all levels, as well as a skills area and amazing views. Owned and supported by the Wellington City Council, the park owes its existence and success to many people, but particularly to its dedicated Supporters' Club, guided by local bikers, the Kennetts.

First developed in 1998, supporters have hand-laid most of the park's 35 km of single track. But they don't only lay track: volunteers have eradicated possums and goats, pulled weeds and planted thousands of trees. The group hopes to re-establish missing or threatened native canopy trees including rimu, rata, tawa, matai and totara, and to attract native birds back to the park with sweet treats such as fuschia, flax, kowhai and cabbage trees.

A trip to the bike park is fun and exciting for anyone who likes to cycle, and bikes are available for hire. Note the donation box.

New Zealand Mountain Bikers' Code
Ride bike and multi-use tracks only.
Ask permission from landowners if necessary.
Respect other users; always give way to walkers.
Leave no trace; never skid or drop rubbish.
Keep your bicycle under control.
Never spook animals; leave gates as you find them.

TRACK DESCRIPTIONS

Koru gentle 2.5 km climb, easy access from the car park to the skills area and beyond

Sally Alley an easy 2 km sidle track

Magic Carpet 600 m easy descent to skills area

Live Wires technical 1 km descent from skills area pylon to car park

SWIGG and Starfish fun 1 km descent to the car park, tricky in parts

Missing Link popular 2 km track sidling down into Nikau Valley and climbing out to a pylon

Ridgeline downhill from the Peak with great views

Zac's Track 1 km narrow track with great views

Trickle Falls 2 km downhill, the hardest in the park, not suited to hard-tails, ride only when dry

Varley's Track 1 km two-way track with lots of switchbacks

Vertigo 1.3 km descent to the bottom of Trickle Falls, steep and gnarly, dry weather only

Leaping Lizard 2 km downhill plus 3 km to car park

Nikau Valley 2 km mostly downhill from the Leaping Lizard end to Missing Link

For an excellent intro to the park, try this 10 km loop (approx two hours): up *Koru*, along *Sally Alley*, through *Missing Link*, up to the top, down the *Ridgeline* and finish off with *SWIGG and Starfish*.

Biking to the park *road route* (40 minutes): from the Cenotaph near Parliament, follow the trolleybus cables up Bowen Street and all the way (7 km) to the end of Karori Road. From the bus turnaround, veer left down South Karori Road for 800 m to the park entrance. *Off-road* (allow two hours): see **Karori Sanctuary Fenceline** and/or **Skyline**.

Hiring bikes at the park Catch the frequent no. 12 Karori Park bus from town to the end of the line, and hire a bike from *Mud Cycles* (see SHOPPING).

OTHER RIDES NEARBY

Karori Sanctuary Fenceline – *Highbury/Brooklyn to Wrights Hill*
This ride (1–2 hours, 10–12 km), affectionately known as the *Rollercoaster*, can be combined with *Skyline* to give an alternative route to the bike park with views and fun aplenty. Novices may need to walk some steep parts, and watch out for other people and their dogs. Simply pick up the fenceline and follow it clockwise: access from *Denton Park* (Highbury Road) or the *wind turbine*. When the track starts to flatten out, look out for the track that peels off to the left and sidles around the *Wright's Hill* summit. Follow it for *Skyline* (and the bike park). Otherwise, keep going to the junction for either the lookout (see CITY LOOKOUTS) or Campbell Street.

Skyline – *Wrights Hill to Fitzgerald Place*
From the lower car park on *Wrights Hill*, follow the road downhill for 500 m until you reach the *Skyline* signpost on your left. This track offers a relatively easy 3.3 km link to the bike park.

Deliverance – *Wrights Hill to Fitzgerald Place*
This is the hardcore alternative to *Skyline*, for grown ups only. This epic (2 km, 15 minute) track took Wellington mountain bikers two years to build.

From Fitzgerald Place to the bike park: ride 100 m down Fitzgerald Place to Hazelwood Ave; turn left and ride 200 m to South Karori Road; turn right and ride 150 m to the car park.

FOR MORE INFORMATION …

Classic New Zealand Mountain Bike Rides, The Kennett Bros & P. Morgan, fifth edition.

Mountain Biking in Wellington City (pamphlet), available from the Wellington City Council or visit **www.feelinggreat.co.nz**

New Zealand Mountain Bike Association, PO Box 13-734, Christchurch, **www.nzmba.org.nz**

For clubs visit **www.mountainbike.co.nz/clubs**

Skating

The smooth, wide-open spaces of the Wellington waterfront make for excellent skating, and there are several options for inline skate hire. For skateboarders, there are lots of dedicated facilities all over town, and you can ride throughout the city, except where signposted, as long as you don't ride 'recklessly or in a manner which may intimidate, be dangerous or cause a nuisance to passersby'.

There are skate parks with assorted obstacles at the following city parks: *Karori Park*, *Wakefield Park* (Island Bay), *Nairnville Park* (Khandallah), *Newlands Park*, *Ian Galloway Park* (Wilton) and alongside *Tawa Pool*.

The *Kilbirnie Recreation Centre* has an indoor skating rink with a range of ramps and inline skate hire (see opposite page).

For waterfront skating, inline skate hire is available from *Ferg's Kayaks*, Queens Wharf. Cost $10 for one hour, $15 for two hours or $25 all day (includes wrist, knee and elbow pads).

For skating gear and repairs, see SHOPPING.

Although he's not one to skate around the issues, Green MP *Nandor Tanczos* rides his skateboard to the seat of national politics. He says hilly Wellington is a great place to skate – but only downhill.

Dominion Post

Swimming Pools and Recreation Centres

The pools and recreation centres listed below are all operated by *Wellington City Council*. Admission charges for all pools (except Khandallah, which is free) are adult $3.50, child (5–14 years, high school pupil with ID) $1.50, child (under 5) 50¢, spectator 50¢, and are open daily 6am–9pm. Summer pools are open summer months only and have different opening hours. Admission charges and opening hours for recreation centres vary.

WELLINGTON REGIONAL AQUATIC CENTRE
63 Kilbirnie Crescent, Kilbirnie, tel 387-8029
Indoor heated 50 m pool, diving well, children's pools, spas, saunas, fitness centre, water and land based fitness classes, swim school, learn to kayak, learn to springboard dive, creche, massage, café and swim shop.

KILBIRNIE RECREATION CENTRE
101 Kilbirnie Crescent, tel 387-1491
A wheel-sport centre with inline skating, skateboarding and roller hockey, etc. The large rink has removable ramps and obstacles, vert and mini half-pipes. *Admission* adult $2, child $1.50, inline skate hire $5. *Open* Fri 3pm–10pm, Sat 11am–2pm (family session, children under 10 only), 2pm–10pm (public session), Sun (alternate Feb–Nov) 10am–2pm (family session, children under 10 only), 2pm–6pm (public session), 6pm–10pm (skateboards only).

FREYBERG POOL AND FITNESS CENTRE
139 Oriental Parade, Oriental Bay, tel 801-4530
Indoor heated 33 m pool, spas, sauna, steam room, fitness centre, and water and land-based fitness and aerobics studio.

KARORI POOL
22 Donald St, Karori, tel 476-5400
Indoor heated, 25 m pool, junior and toddlers pool, spa, swim school and aquafitness.

KARORI RECREATION CENTRE
251 Karori Road, tel 476-8090
A multi-use gymnasium with ball sport markings and a squash court. Casual bookings welcome.

THORNDON SUMMER POOL

26 Murphy Street, Thorndon, tel 472-8055
Outdoor, heated, 30 m pool. Open Labour Day–Easter, Mon–Fri
6.30am–7pm, Sat/Sun 8.30am–6.30pm, late nights Mon/Wed 8pm.

KHANDALLAH SUMMER POOL

Woodmancote Road, Khandallah, tel 479-6644
Outdoor 30 m pool plus toddlers pool (both unheated) next to
Khandallah Park. Open late Nov–Mar 10am–6pm.

NAIRNVILLE RECREATION CENTRE

Corner Cockayne Road and Lucknow Terrace, Khandallah, tel 479-2022
Full size basketball court, squash court. Casual bookings welcome.

KEITH SPRY POOL

15 Frankmoore Ave, Johnsonville, tel 478-9237
Indoor heated 25 m pool, toddlers pool, diving pool, spa, sauna,
aquafitness, swim school, massage, leisure and barbecue area.

NEWLANDS RECREATION CENTRE

Newlands College, Bracken Road, tel 478-6524
Full size court and spectator area suitable for most indoor pursuits
plus two squash courts and a fitness/weights room. Open for public
use after 5pm Mon–Fri and all other non-school times.

TAWA POOL

Davies Street, Tawa, tel 232-7041
Indoor heated 25 m pool, learners and toddlers pool, spa, sauna,
swim school and aquafitness.

H2O Xtreme

Corner Blenheim & Brown Streets, Upper Hutt, tel 527-2113,
www.h2oxtream.com
Swirl in the rapids, ride the waves and take donuts down the
slide at Upper Hutt's special pool! Grown-up swimming in the
25 m lane pool, plus sauna, spa and steam room. *Admission* adult
$4, children (under 14) $3, (under 5) $2.50. Open Mon–Thurs
6am–9pm, Fri 6am–10pm, Sat/Sun 8am–9pm.

Bays and Beaches

A tour of the bays is Wellington's classic drive, but makes an even better bicycle ride (bikes can be hired from *Penny Farthing* in Courtenay Place) with a complete circuit taking around 3 hours. On a hot summer day, pack your picnic and head straight for the beach. The water's not that cold! It's actually a very reasonable 15°C (59°F)! All are safe for bathing except those near the harbour entrance and on the south coast.

A *clockwise* highlights tour, starting from Oriental Bay…

Weightlifting (!) at Oriental Bay, 1955.

Alexander Turnbull Library, Wellington, New Zealand, F-57016-1/2.

ORIENTAL BAY

Welcome to Wellington's promenade. On any sunny day, you'll see scores of walkers, joggers, skaters, sunbathers and cyclists. The bay is named after the *Oriental*, which sailed from London in September 1839 with 155 settlers, reaching Wellington on 31 January 1840.

About 100 m off the beach is the *Carter Fountain*, built in the early 1970s. The *Band Rotunda* was built in 1936 as a changing pavilion for swimmers, and in the early 1980s the top floor was enclosed and turned into a restaurant. The ground floor now houses the *Wellington Arts Centre* where you can view displays on the history of the Bay.

The beach you see before you, though, was radically transformed in 2003. This major redevelopment has seen the creation of the pier and tidal pool, given us more grass and, most importantly, 27,000 tonnes of beautiful golden sand (thank you Takaka!).

The Famous Crocodile
Chaffers Marina (next to Overseas Passenger Terminal), tel 902-2243
This is fun for family and friends! Cruise Wellington's
waterfront on a two- or four-seater covered four-wheel bicycle.
Cost two-seater: $10/half hour, $15/hour; four-seater: $18/half
hour, $25/hour. Open weekends and public holidays from 10am,
weather permitting.

BALAENA BAY
A sheltered bay with sand and stones, good for swimming. Toilets
and shower, ramp access to beach and car park alongside.

HATAITAI BEACH
Another sheltered bay with facilities including a large bathing
deck. Grassy picnic spot opposite.

SCORCHING BAY
A busy beach in the summer with glamour, golden sand, good
swimming and a large lawn for lounging around. Toilets, changing
rooms and cold shower. A visit to the *Chocolate Fish* café will be
worth the queue.

WORSER BAY
A long sandy beach with a ski lane and boat ramp. Picnic benches,
cold shower, changing rooms and toilets (open summer only).
Windsurfing classes are held here in the summer (see SEA SPORTS).

SEATOUN BEACH
A shingle beach with boat ramp, ski lane and a popular pier for
fishing and leaping off. Churchill Park can be found at the eastern
end: playground, picnic spots, cold shower and toilets. The park is
also home to the *Wahine* anchor (see **Eastern Walkway**).

BREAKER BAY
Dramatic and interesting, Breaker Bay is a fantastic arc flanked
by craggy outcrops, opening out to an expanse of sea. Nudists.
Parking.

LYALL BAY
Surfer's Paradise, or at least it soon will be – see SEA SPORTS.

PRINCESS BAY AND HOUGHTON BAY
Rock pool adventure and a grand view of Te Waka a Maui, the South Island. Fearless surfers provide spine-chilling entertainment in high seas. Car park and toilets. The *Southern Walkway* starts/ends here.

ISLAND BAY
A quaint bay with a postcard view of Taputeranga Island with fishing boats in the foreground. Playground and café nearby. An easy and pleasant bus journey. Don't miss the summertime *Whopper Chopper*.

OWHIRO BAY
Rugged 'red rocks', the gateway to *Te Kopahou Reserve* (see SCENIC RESERVES). To get back to town from here, follow Owhiro Road.

Across the harbour, *Days Bay* has a good beach and a perfect pier for leaping off.

Go to the *Kapiti Coast* for an expanse of golden sand.

Wellington Arts Centre
The basement of the beachside Band Rotunda in Oriental Bay is home to the *Wellington Arts Centre* (tel 385-1929, email arts@wcc.govt.nz), open to the public for a wide range of events. The centre has an interesting display of local historical photos, and while you're there, check out the range of courses on offer – most with a creative focus – music and drama, visual arts for children and adults, plus a community darkroom for hire. The *Wellington Photographic Society* meets here, as does the *Storytellers' Café* and *Folk Music Club*, and the office is shared with Wellington's established *International Jazz Festival* and the emerging *International Poetry Festival*. There's plenty on offer for anyone who wants to get their creative energy flowing, and you'll meet some nice people too. For more information visit **www.feelinggreat.co.nz/arts**.

Sea Sports

Wellington Harbour is a busy port and popular for sport and recreation. The enclosed shape gives many sheltered bays regardless of wind direction, and the exposed south coast provides diving and fishing opportunities.

There's enough room in the inner harbour for all aquatic activities, and on any given day you might see a bit of everything: yachts racing, pleasure boats cruising, kayaks, fishing from the pier or boat, divers, swimmers and fossickers. There are several marinas and boat ramps, as well as waterski lanes, jet ski, surfing and windsurfing areas. For those who like it salty, there's much to satisfy you here.

Dominion Post

FERG'S KAYAKS

Shed 6, Queens Wharf, tel 499-8898, www.fergskayaks.co.nz
Kayak hire for harbour paddling, plus coaching for sea, multi-sport and white water kayaking. Owner Ian Ferguson is a watersports legend – veteran of five Olympic Games (four gold, one silver), two world kayaking titles, four times New Zealand Ironman Champion, plus numerous other titles in sprint kayaking, surf lifesaving, surf ski and paddle board racing, so he ought to be getting pretty good at it by now. *Cost* single kayak $12 one our, $18 two hours. *Open* daily.

LIVING SIMPLY

295 Jackson Street, Petone, tel 939-1133, www.livingsimply.co.nz
Double kayak hire for enjoying the Hutt River, Petone foreshore, or mission to Eastbourne or Matiu/Somes. One way by arrangement. *Cost* $60 double kayak full day. *Open* daily from 10am.

Whale Watch

Wellington Harbour is teeming with marine life, and whales, sharks and dolphins are regular visitors. Our easily accessible coastline offers good vantage points for viewing spectacular displays by frolicking dolphins or pods of orca. In fact, these displays have proven problematic when rubbernecking motorists stop to watch!

The harbour used to be a popular calving area for the less common southern right whale and they are occasionally seen cruising the waters of the inner harbour, a long way from the sub-Antarctic waters where they calve these days. In 1999 a rare visit to the harbour proved fatal for a 5 m scamperdown whale, which was found washed up next to the ferry terminal. The usual habitat of the scamperdown is deep water beyond the continental shelf and visits to coastal waters are rare.

See www.whalewatch.co.nz for photos and more information, or for general background, see www.wdcs.org – the site of the international *Whale and Dolphin Conservation Society*.

ROYAL PORT NICHOLSON YACHT CLUB SAILING ACADEMY

115 Oriental Parade, tel 382-8152, www.sailingacademy.org.nz
Two purpose-built yachts for sailing training offer an exciting yet forgiving environment for beginners to experienced sailors. Cruising and racing options, dinghy training and coastguard studies. Learn to sail courses run year-round.

DOLPHIN SAILING ACADEMY

Berth 2, Pier E, Chaffers Marina, tel 586-0699, www.dolphinsailing.co.nz
Harbour cruises and learn to sail packages. Wet weather clothing and all lifejackets are provided. Fishing and dinner charters on offer, as are sailing holidays and sailing programmes in the Marlborough Sounds.

WORSER BAY BOATING CLUB

Marine Parade, Seatoun, tel 972-3326, www.wbbc.wellington.net.nz
'The Worser the Bay, the better the sailing.' Small boat sailing for all ages. Optimists, P Class, Starlings, Lasers, OK Dinghies and Sunbursts. New members welcome. Learn to sail courses run Oct–April; regular racing on Saturdays.

For more on Wellington yacht clubs, see www.wya.wellington.net.nz

H2OSPORTS WINDSURFING CENTRE

Marine Parade, Worser Bay, tel 388-6164, www.h2osports.co.nz
Windsurfing lessons, beginners to advanced. Gear for short- and
long-term hire. Kite-surfing also available. *Open* summer only.

Local Diving Spots

The most popular local dive sites are the South Coast, Makara and
the Mana/Kapiti area, between them offering diving opportunities
whatever the winds or swell. There's a diversity of marine life,
including crayfish and paua. Temperatures range from 10–18°C, and
visibility averages 5–8 m, but can reach as much as 25 m.

ISLAND BAY DIVERS

Corner of Reef Street & The Parade, Island Bay, tel 383-6778,
www.ibdivers.co.nz
Owners Tim and Irene Walsh have decades of diving experience
and you'll find them helpful and knowledgeable. The shop hires
snorkel and scuba equipment, trains all levels of divers and runs
trips by boat, shore or road. It's a PADI Dive Centre and NAUI
Career Training Centre. They also retail and service many popular
equipment brands, as well as doing air fills and tank testing. Dive
Club meets 9am on Sat. *Open* (summer) Mon–Fri 10am–7pm, Sat/Sun
9am–6pm; (winter) same hours but closed Tues/Wed.

SPLASH GORDON'S DIVE SPECIALISTS

432 The Esplanade, Island Bay, tel 939-3483, www.splashgordon.co.nz
A PADI five-star dive facility offering full dive training through to
instructor level. Boat charters available every weekend on a purpose-
built dive boat; weekday trips by arrangement. Full retail outlet
with popular brands plus a wide range of spear-fishing equipment.
Air fills, nitrox and gear hire available. Dive club. Trips available to
popular New Zealand dive spots including The Poor Knights, White
Island and wreck of the Mikhail Lermontov. *Open* Mon–Fri 8.30am–
5.30pm, Sat/Sun 8am–5.30pm.

For more on diving, try
www.divespots.co.nz
www.nznz.co.nz/scuba-diving-snorkelling

Surf's Up!

Lyall Bay in Wellington has a long history of surfing and has been called 'the origin of modern surfing in New Zealand'. Less than 15 minutes from downtown Wellington, the bay has excellent potential for surfing because the wind blows mostly offshore and there's usually an underlying swell. However, the gently shelving nature of the sand means the waves 'close-out' over most of the bay. The best break in the Bay requires a large swell, and can get over-crowded.

But that's all about to change! Local surfers, recognising the potential to use artificial surfing reef technology, formed the **Lyall Bay Reef Trust** to lobby and fund raise for an artificial reef in the bay. In 2003, the Trust received the good news that resource consent had been granted, and that means construction could begin as early as the summer of 2004 if the necessary funds can be raised and sand can be sourced for the reef's 'geotextile bags'.

The reef will provide 200m of rideable wave face, and is expected to increase the number of quality surfing days from 27 to between 118 and 142 per annum. Tony Lines, Reef Trust chairman, says 'the reef has been designed to provide both a challenging right and left break which will include fast steep sections as well as a tube ride and barrel in surf of between 0.75 m and 4.5 m. It will be a thrill for competent surfers when the swell is up and rideable by all when it's small.' *For more information*, visit **www.lyallbayreef.org.nz**

OTHER SURFING SPOTS

Our advice for safe and enjoyable surfing in Wellington is *make friends with the locals* and *know your territory*. The south coast gets a lot of southerly swell, causing small breaks to appear, but it can be a dangerous place to surf with its submerged rocks and unpredictable rips. For details on south coast surfing spots, visit **www.maranui.co.nz** and follow the *surf map* link.

Other surfing spots up to two hours further afield in the Wairarapa include Palliser Bay (Ocean Beach, Lake Ferry, Ning Nong, Dee Dees), White Rock (the Spit), Tora, Uriti Point, Riversdale and Castlepoint (Slipperys, the Gap, Christmas Tree Bay).

For weather, see the daily *Dominion Post* or visit **www.metservice.co.nz**

Adventure and Adrenaline

FERG'S KAYAKS
Shed 6, Queens Wharf, tel 499-8898, www.fergskayaks.co.nz
New Zealand's largest indoor real rock climbing wall. Try
ledges, cracks, aretes and overhangs, or abseiling in a safe, fun
environment. For the novice and expert alike, everyone gets to have
a go, aided by experienced staff. Cost from $5. Open daily.

TOP ADVENTURES AND HANGDOG INDOOR CLIMBING CENTRE
453 Hutt Road, Lower Hutt, tel 589-9181
Rock climb on New Zealand's highest indoor climbing wall, plus
a range of adventure activities such as caving, rafting, abseiling,
bridge swinging, canyoning, sea kayaking and rap jumping. Cost rock
climbing $9, other adventures $50–$200. Open daily 9am–9pm.

BUNGY EXTREME
Corner Taranaki Street & Courtenay Place, tel 382-8438
'Reaching Wellington's outer limits,' this is the bungy for those
who are too scared to jump. Up to three passengers are catapulted
together in a capsule 55 m into the air at speeds reaching 160 km/h
in less than two seconds. Lots of fun, inexpensive, and only two
people have ever vomited. Cost per person $35. Open daily 12pm–late
(weather permitting).

PENCARROW STATION HORSE TREKKING
1320 Coast Road, Wainuiomata, tel 564-8805
A wonderful scenic horse trek with breathtaking coastal views,
native bush and hidden lakes. Cost two hours $40, three hours $60.
Telephone for bookings.

COUNTRY CLUB RIDING ACADEMY
517 Ohariu Valley Road, Ohariu, tel 478-8472, www.horsetrekking.co.nz
A visit to the stables is an excellent excuse to drive through the
picturesque Ohariu Valley. Horse treks and arena riding for riders
of all ages and abilities – '… a high quality experience, great
staff and a professional, safety conscious way of operating' says
Vivienne. Treks of varying lengths run during the weekends;
moonlight treks by arrangement. Cost adult $30–$80, child $16–$40.
There's a café and play area open to the public Fri/Sat/Sun.

Indoor Fun

BOWLAND PORIRUA
35 Kenepuru Drive, Porirua, tel 237-4428, www.bowland.co.nz
Twenty lanes with learn to bowl classes plus glow in the dark
bowling. Casual players welcome. Bar and café on site. Cost before
11am $6 per game; after 11am: 1st game $9.50, 2nd game $6, 3rd
game $4.50 (includes shoe hire). Open daily 9am–midnight.

TENPIN PETONE
12 Western Hutt Road, Petone, tel 568-3168, www.tenpinpetone.co.nz
Twenty lanes with bar, café, big screen TV, gaming and amusement
machines and pool table. Any size group welcome. Cost adult $8,
child $6. Open daily 9am–midnight.

TIMEOUT XTREME
127 Manners Street, 384-4955
A video games parlour offering a large variety of up-to-date high-
tech games. Its second branch at 15 Courtenay Place (incorporating
Laser Force, below) has more children's games including air hockey,
plus a good value Wednesday night $10 all you can play session
6pm–8pm.

LASER FORCE
15 Courtenay Place, tel 384-4622, www.laserforcenz.co.nz
Armed with a laser force phaser and a vest style battle-suit, your
mission is to destroy the opponents' force field generator and zap the
other team as many times as you can, while trying to avoid getting
zapped yourself (although everyone gets to live to the end. Hooray!).
You attack and defend in a bizarre maze with lights, smoke and
music all adding to the excitement, or confusion! Everything is fully
automated and computerised. Suitable for all ages, but probably best
for children over 8. Costs are around adult $18, child $12 (3 games);
minimum 5 people per group. Book in advance.

INDOOR GRAND PRIX
2 Westminster Street, Kaiwharawhara, tel 499-0676, www.karting.co.nz
Indoor carting. Start your engines and zoom around the track just
inches from the ground on these speedy go-karts. Great fun for
children aged 7 years and older. Ride alone, or go with friends and

family for a grand prix event. It's a chance to prove that you're as good a driver as you say you are. Children over 1.2 m tall only. *Cost* $1 per minute per driver. *Open* daily 10am–9.30pm.

DAYTONA INDOOR RACEWAY

43b Seaview Road, Old Ford Factory, Lower Hutt, tel 586-8632, www.daytona.co.nz
New Zealand's largest track and the fastest indoor go-karts. Ideal for families, friends and social clubs. Children over 8 years old only. *Costs* from adult $18.50, child $12, spectators free. Book in advance. *Open* daily.

Ball Sports

KARORI GOLF CLUB

South Makara Road, Makara, tel 476-7337, www.karorigolf.co.nz
A great 18-hole course close to town (25-minute drive), in a pleasant rural setting. Visitors welcome, with club hire available. *Green fees* Mon–Fri $25, Sat/Sun $35. Telephone for a tee time.

WAINUIOMATA GOLF CLUB

334 Coast Road, Wainuiomata, tel 564-7746, www.wainuigolf.co.nz
A hidden jewel in a picturesque valley, around 30 minutes drive from the city. This interesting 18-hole course is a pleasure to play with its tree-lined fairways and excellent greens. An easily walked, lush course all year round. Golf shop, driving range, club hire. *Green fees* Mon–Fri $20, Sat/Sun $30. Telephone for a tee time.

PARAPARAUMU BEACH GOLF CLUB

376 Kapiti Road, Paraparaumu Beach, tel (04) 902-8200, www.paraparaumubeachgolfclub.co.nz
Paraparaumu Beach Links is rated as one of the best courses in New Zealand and ranks 95th in the world. The well-drained undulating fairways, fierce rough, fast greens and intimidating bunkers combine with the naturally windy coastal weather to create a wonderful golfing challenge. Around 40 minutes drive from Wellington City. Visitors welcome. Telephone (well in advance) for a tee time. *Green fees* $90.

Tiger Woods woz 'ere!

The 2002 New Zealand Golf Open held at Paraparaumu Beach Golf Club played host to the world's no. 1 golfer, Tiger Woods. His arrival caused quite a stir! While some grumbled about his rumoured NZ$5 million appearance fee, most were thrilled to see a golfer of such high stature visit our shores, and many were grateful for the opportunity to watch him in action. His caddy is local boy Steve Williams, a man with many sporting strings to his bow. When he takes a break from the bag, he can sometimes be seen driving at the Wellington Speedway, of which he is a member and keen supporter.

SHANDON GOLF COURSE

Gear Island, Jackson Street, Petone, tel 939-6308, www.shandongolf.co.nz
A par 70, 18-hole course – not overly difficult in length but truely challenging by design. The club provides complete practice facilities with practice chipping and putting greens, and practice fairways. The course will test the skill of any golfer without unfairly leaving out the beginner. *Green fees* $40-$60. Visitors can play most days; telephone for a tee time.

HUTT GOLF CLUB

Military Road, Lower Hutt, tel 567-4722
Smack in the middle of Lower Hutt, this 18-hole course is the oldest in the North Island, and considered by some to be underrated. Fairway watering ensures lush fairways all year round; the course is flat and easy walking. The facilities including pro shop and restaurant are excellent. Resident professional, club hire. *Green fees* $40. Open to visitors Mon–Fri; telephone for a tee time.

BERHAMPORE GOLF COURSE

Adelaide Road, Berhampore, tel 389-6685
The closest to downtown Wellington, this 18-hole municipal course borders the Town Belt, about 10 minutes drive from the city centre. Inexpensive and hilly; not for the faint-hearted! *Green fees* Mon–Fri $10, Sat/Sun $15, concessions for children. Visitors always welcome.

OHARIU VALLEY GOLF CLUB

Ohariu Valley Road, Ohariu Valley, Johnsonville, tel 478-4009
A pleasant, undulating 9-hole course about 35 minutes from the
city, situated in a peaceful rural valley (access via Karori/Makara or
Johnsonville). *Green fees* (18 holes) $20. Visitors always welcome.

MAKARA PUBLIC GOLF COURSE

386 Makara Road, Makara, tel 476-6854
This casual, picturesque 9-holf course has probably seen more first-
time players than any other in the region, being both inexpensive
and relaxed. And you never know what you'll see – a stray sheep
nibbling at the rough, perhaps snowy white ducks hanging out by
the green. A little rugged in places with some unpredictable greens,
the course is otherwise totally playable and its relative shortness
makes for effortless, pleasant golfing – the way all golf should be!
No gumboots. Club hire. *Green fees* (9 holes) Mon–Fri $7, Sat/Sun $8.

TITAHI BAY GOLF CLUB

Gloaming Hill, Titahi Bay, tel 236-7324
A good excuse to visit Titahi Bay. This casual 9-hole course is hilly
and challenging, but spectacular sea views make it special. *Green fees*
$10. Visitors always welcome.

RENOUF TENNIS CENTRE

Brooklyn Road, tel 385-9709
Four indoor and 14 outdoor tennis courts open to the public. Private
bookings available; resident coach on site; tennis shop, bar and café.
Cost indoor $30–36 per hour, outdoor $12–16 per hour. *Open* daily from
8am.

CLUB K

73 Salamanca Road, Kelburn, tel 472-9299, www.clubk.co.nz
Ten freshly refurbished squash courts available from $5 per person,
plus gymnasium facilities, golf nets ($4 for 50 balls), table tennis,
pro shop, massage, sauna and tanning. Casual visitors welcome, with
equipment hire available including rackets and mountain bikes.
Telephone for bookings; concessions and membership packages
available. *Open* Mon–Thurs 6.30am–10pm, Fri 6.30am–8pm, Sat 9am–
7pm, Sun 9am–9pm.

Spectator Sports

WESTPAC STADIUM

Waterloo Quay, tel 473-3881, www.westpacstadium.co.nz

The 34,500-seat Westpac Stadium opened in January 2000 and has since played host to a wide variety of sporting and cultural events. We think it's fantastic. You can't beat the atmosphere when it's full of happy people having fun. And when there's a big event on, the city is all a-buzz. Evening events see the city sky aglow with the stadium's lights, and later on the crowds disperse into downtown Wellington for post-match analysis or a bit of a party.

Facilities include food and drink outlets, merchandise stands, ATMs and the Pavilion public bar, decorated with pictures of sports heroes and a stadium history display. There are wheelchair and baby-change facilities too.

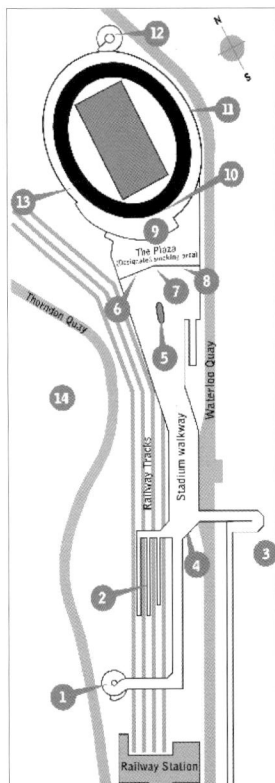

1. Main pedestrian access from Thorndon Quay

2. Access from Railway platforms.

3. Pedestrian access from port and Lambton Harbour areas.

4. Entrance to carpark and entry for taxis and disabled persons.

5. Ticket pick-up booth.

6. Main entry gate for tickets in aisles 1 to 18

7. Ticket sales both for event day.

8. Main entry gate for aisles 19 to 36. Entrance for Rugby Season ticket holders.

9. Stadium entrance.

10. Automatic teller machine.

11. Entry tunnels to aisles 19 to 36.

12. Emergency exit only at the northern end behind the replay screen.

13. Entry tunnels to aisles 1 to 18.

There's plenty of rugby played at the stadium. During the **Super 12** season (late Feb–May) the **Hurricanes** play most of their home games here, and during the NPC season (Aug–Oct) the stadium is home to the **Wellington Lions**. For fixtures, see www.wellingtonrugby.co.nz.

There's *cricket* in summer – the **New Zealand Black Caps** often play their one-day international matches here (tests are usually played at the Basin Reserve). For fixtures, see www.nzcricket.co.nz.

On the *entertainment* front, the stadium hosts all sorts of events including pop concerts and annual lifestyle shows such as the **Home and Garden Show** and the **Food Show**.

Tickets to rugby union events are available from *Red Tickets* (**www.redtickets.co.nz**, tel 0800-000-575) or from *New Zealand Post* and Books & More shops. For all other events, tickets are sold by *Ticketek* (Cuba/Wakefield Street intersection, **www.ticketek.com**, tel 384-3840) and gate sales are sometimes available, usually two hours prior to the event. For more information about events and ticketing, visit the stadium's website.

WELLINGTON SPEEDWAY

SH2, Te Marua, Upper Hutt, tel 0900-93366, www.wellingtonspeedway.co.nz
Fast paced, thrilling motor racing action from high-speed super saloons and modifieds, hard-hitting stockcars, sidecar madness and street-stocks. If you're lucky, you'll see the caravan demolition derby – you'll laugh your socks off. Coffee and hot food available including the venerable hot-dog-on-a-stick. Rug up warm and prepare for dust. *Entry* adult $12, secondary students with ID $8, child $5, under 5s free, family $30 (2 adults/4 children). *Meetings* most Saturdays Oct–April, 7pm start. Check the website or ring for dates.

WELLINGTON RACING CLUB

Racecourse Road, Trentham, Upper Hutt, tel 528-9611, www.trentham.co.nz
A day at the races! Trentham has racing around once a month, and the highlight of the season is *Wellington Cup Day* in January, the showcase raceday with many special events including *Fashion in the Field* and top quality racing. Race meets start at noon except winter meetings (11am start). Facilities include totes, bars and restaurants.

Sightseeing Tours

WELLINGTON ROVER

Tel 021-426-211, www.wellingtonrover.co.nz

Explore Wellington City and its coastline. The Rover does a circuit taking in all Wellington's coastal attractions including the Massey Memorial, Scorching Bay, and Red Rocks and the Sinclair Head seal colony, and the Rover Day Pass ($35) allows 'hop on, hop off' exploration of whatever takes your fancy. The Rover Ring Tour ($150) takes you to seven Lord of the Rings film locations including Rivendell, and the Twilight Rover Tour ($30) is their winter evening tour. Expect friendly service and lively commentary from Jason and his team on these small group sightseeing tours.

WELLESLEY HARBOUR CRUISE SHIP

Departs from Taranaki Street Wharf (next to Circa Theatre), tel 474-1308

The Wellesley, a tastefully restored 40m-long heritage vessel, offers a chance to tour the harbour in comfort while enjoying light meals, tea and coffee, and a fully licensed bar service. This is a popular attraction, considered by many to be excellent value for money. One-hour afternoon cruises Sat/Sun 1pm, 2pm and 3pm ($3); dinner cruises with live music on Fri/Sat 6.30pm ($45) or stay onboard for the night and have breakfast as well ($69, share twin). All sailings are weather dependent.

HAMMOND'S WELLINGTON SIGHTSEEING TOURS

Tel 472-0869, www.wellingtonsightseeingtours.com

Three tours daily, all year round: Wellington City Sights & Coastline ($40–$50) visits all major city attractions including Parliament, Botanic Garden, Old St Pauls, Cable Car and Mt Victoria lookout. Kapiti Gold Coast ($65–$75) takes you to the seaside town of Plimmerton, Pauatahanui Inlet, Lindale Farm (animals, cheeses/ice cream, shopping), car museum, chocolate factory and the Paekakariki Hill summit for views of Kapiti and South Island. The full-day Wairarapa Wine, Seals & Palliser Bay tour ($130–$140) includes *Lord of the Rings* film sites, farmscapes, a fell engine and the quaint towns and wine-tasting of the Wairarapa.

FLAT EARTH NEW ZEALAND EXPERIENCES

Tel 0800-775-805 or 977-5805, www.flatearth.co.nz

Upmarket and unique exploration in small, friendly groups. The *Capital Arts* tour focuses on Wellington's vibrant, eclectic art and architecture. Inspiration is an unforgettable journey around the city's dramatic highlights. *Wild Wellington* shows Wellington's extraordinary natural features and contrasts. *Your City Tour* is a custom-built tour depending on your timeframe and interests. Cost per person for full day packages $210, or custom tours from $120. Tour price covers all entry fees, morning/afternoon tea, lunch and accommodation pick-ups and drop-offs.

DYNAMIC TOURS

Tel 801-6900, www.dynamictours.co.nz

Susie and Paul have been offering tours in Wellington for more than 10 years, and pride themselves on exceptional service. They'll show you the harbour, the hills, the city and the sea, and offer customised tours such as gardens, farming, golf, fishing, cultural and cuisine. Cost range $84–$107, and tours open all year around at times to suit.

FIVE STAR TOURS

Tel 479-1356

Escorted sightseeing tours throughout Wellington, the Kapiti Coast and Wairarapa for individuals and groups. Martinborough winery tours a speciality: visit several boutique wineries for tastings and an opportunity to purchase. Also trips to Mount Bruce National Wildlife Centre. Call David Simon for details. Cost $50–$150.

HELILINK

George Bolt Street, Wellington Airport, tel 0800-435-454, www.helilink.co.nz

A range of scenic flights over the city and harbour and as far afield as the Marlborough Sounds. Also offer transport/activity packages such as heli-golf, heli-wine trails, heli-fishing, and heli-dining.

HELIPRO

Queens Wharf, tel 0800-CHOPPER, www.helipro.co.nz

Scenic flights, lunch dates, lodge transfers. Cost from $75.

Shopping

SHOPPING

Wellington is packed with fantastic shops, many still family owned and independent. And as you'll soon discover, there are far too many to mention here. So we asked our insiders where they shopped and why, and the resulting selection presents the tried and true retailers of Wellington City. These consistent performers boast of an incredibly satisfying and fun shopping experience, with their amazing range of high quality goods, well displayed and delivered with a smile. The emphasis here is on local products – the things unique to Wellington and many found only in New Zealand.

Most of these shops lie close together in the inner city, so shopping on foot is easy and pleasant. Regular bus services will take you to the outer shopping villages such as Newtown, Thorndon and Petone. Frequent coffee stops are highly recommended.

The sequence of shops within each section is city-centre first, followed by those further afield. Most are open Monday–Friday 9am–5.30pm, with some open for late night shopping on Friday until 7–8pm. Almost all are open on the weekends, and public holiday hours are similar to Sundays.

Gifts, Souvenirs and Art

TE PAPA STORE
At Te Papa, Cable Street, tel 381-7013, www.tepapastore.co.nz
Te Papa Store is one of the best places in town for fairly priced New
Zealand-made gifts and souvenirs. Every possibility and price range
is covered including some stunning glassware, woodcarving and
hand-painted silks. Books, confectionery and other small gifts too.
Open Mon–Wed 9.30am–6pm, Thurs 9.30am–9pm, Fri–Sun 9.30am–6pm.

THE POTTERS SHOP AND GALLERY
1st Floor, Capital on the Quay, 226 Lambton Quay, tel 473-8803
The Potters Shop and Gallery is a co-operative founded in 1984 and
its reputation for beautiful handcrafted work is well known at
home and abroad. This is the largest range of quality pottery in
Wellington, plus hand-painted silk, turned wood and jewellery.
Open Mon–Thurs 9am–5.30pm, Fri 9am–6pm, Sat/Sun 10am–4pm.

SOMMERFIELDS
296 Lambton Quay, tel 499-4847, www.sommerfields.net
Gifts and furniture, some unique and exclusive to the store. All New
Zealand-made from natural products: native woods, wool, lamb and
possum skin, paua shell, bone and greenstone. Glass and pottery
artworks by talented craftspeople. A well presented selection. *Open
Mon–Thurs 9am–5.30pm, Fri 9am–6pm, Sat 10am–5pm, Sun 11am–4pm.*

THE VAULT
1st Floor, 50 Willis Street, tel 471-1404
Unique gifts, funky clocks, stylish watches, an extensive selection
of New Zealand-made jewellery and other designer items from
home and abroad. It has been said more than once – 'something for
everyone'. Great browsing in an ambient, otherworldly interior.
Open Mon–Fri 9am–6pm, Sat 10am–5pm, Sun 11am–3pm.

SIMPLY NEW ZEALAND
Visitor Centre, Civic Square, tel 802-4422
A handy location next to the Visitor Information Centre, with all
the staple souvenirs you'd expect – postcards, paua shell and All
Blacks apparel. *Open Mon–Fri 9am–5.30pm, Sat/Sun 10am–4pm.*

Affordable and Collectable Art

If you're interested in browsing or acquiring artwork, the dealer galleries listed below are for you. They boast of a lively arts scene, with plenty of talent and originality on show. In many styles and any media, for appreciation or for sale, expect to see plenty of exciting work – painting, photography, glass, ceramics, sculpture, jewellery and more.

Most are open Mon–Sat from 10am. Thursday's *Dominion Post* has details of their special exhibits, as does the *Capital Times*.

Tinakori Gallery, 132 Featherston Street, Thorndon
Millwood Gallery, 291b Tinakori Road, Thorndon
Woodhouse Hill Gallery, 344 Tinakori Road, Thorndon
McGregor Wright Gallery, 26 Waring Taylor Street
Ferner Galleries, 128 Featherston Street
Art Works of New Zealand, 117 Customhouse Quay
Hamish McKay Gallery, 1st Floor, 50 Willis Street
Sulu Gallery, 53 Boulcott Street
Avid, 48 Victoria Street
Tamarillo, 102 Wakefield Street
Roar! Gallery, 22 Vivian Street
Peter McLeavey Gallery, 147 Cuba Street
Bartley Nees Gallery, 147 Cuba Street
Janne Land Gallery, Furness Lane
Bowen Galleries & CM Moore Gallery, 35 Ghuznee Street
Art's OK, 38 Ghuznee Street
The Walrus Gallery, 111 Taranaki Street
Photospace studio/gallery, 1st floor, 37 Courtenay Place
Kura Gallery, 19 Allen Street
Emerge Gallery, Corner Wakefield & Chaffers Streets
Idiom Studio, 26 Elizabeth Street, Mt Victoria
Naxos Art Exhibits, 24 Tacey Street, Kilbirnie
Milk Gallery, 8 Rimu Street, Eastbourne
Rona Fine Arts, 17 Rimu Street, Eastbourne
Williams Gallery, 326 Jackson Street, Petone
Lewis–Paape Gallery, 330 High Street, Lower Hutt

SHOPPING

BELLO
140 Willis Street, tel 385-0058, www.bello.co.nz
Bello is sumptuous. This lovely little shop stocks luxuries such
as New Zealand-made bed linen and French handbags (what a
combination!). With a quality rather than quantity approach to its
stock, you'll be lucky to find a better selection of beautiful things
under one small roof. *Open Mon–Thurs 10am–6pm, Fri 10am–8pm, Sat/Sun
10am–4pm.*

D.VICE
Corner Willis & Dixon Streets, tel 384-1505, www.dvice.co.nz
Quality sex gear for adventurous everyday people (as long as they're
over 18). A lengthy offering of own-brand, New Zealand-made adult
toys; some imported goodies available. *Open Tues–Thurs 10am–6pm, Fri
10am–7pm, Sat 11am–5pm, Sun 11am–4pm.*

TRADE AID
74 Cuba Street, tel 385-4498, www.tradeaid.com
Fairly traded homeware, furnishings, jewellery, gifts, tea and
coffee, and a mountain of other goods. Trade Aid gives priority to
suppliers who work with the disadvantaged, ensure child labour is
not used detrimentally and employ sustainable production methods
and materials. *Open Mon–Thurs 9am–6pm, Fri 9am–9pm, Sat 10am–4pm, Sun
11am–4pm.*

IKO IKO
118 Cuba Mall, tel 385-0977, www.ikoiko.co.nz
A shop where the tastful and tacky collide, Iko Iko is brimming
with funky gifts for your friends. From the delicious kitsch of a
wind-up flashing peacock to the serenity of a scented feng shui
candle, Iko Iko caters for every taste, with goods from all over the
globe. *Open Mon–Thurs 9.30am–5.30pm, Fri 9.30am–8pm, Sat 10am–4.30pm, Sun
11am–4pm.*

RED CURRENT
14–16 Allen Street, tel 803–3432
For the unique and unusual. Perfect pressies for any occasion
including homeware, accessories, furniture and beauty products.
Open Mon–Thurs 9.30am–5.30pm, Fri 9am–7.30pm, Sat 10am–4pm, Sun 11am–3pm.

Fashion, Jewellery and Leather

The Wellington fashion scene is flourishing, with a growing number of local and national designers setting up shop in the inner city. As their labels gain popularity both at home and abroad, local folk scamble for the pick of exciting new season stock. You too can wear the classiest Kiwi cuts and be the envy of your friends by shopping at the best of our boutiques, following below.

SHOPPING

UNITYCOLLECTION
101 Customhouse Quay, tel 471-1008, www.unitycollection.co.nz
An award-winning boutique with beautiful clothes for the stylish woman. Here is some of the best that New Zealand has to offer in high fashion and new generation designers including Carlson, Kate Sylvester, Mild Red, Natalija Kucija, State of Grace and Trelise Cooper. Take a fat purse. *Open Mon–Thurs 10am–6pm, Fri 10am–7pm, Sat 10am–4.30pm, Sun 11am–4pm.*

ZFA
111 Customhouse Quay, tel 499-0408
ZFA's designs are defined by a spare aesthetic, directional clean lines and long, lean silhouettes. Wellingtonian Zana Feuchs has been designing for more than 14 years, and offers custom fitting – great for women who can't find trousers that fit. ZFA also stocks Strong, Deborah Sweeney, Lois Phin, Insidious Fix, Cybele, Aesop and Sisley. *Open Mon–Fri 10am–5.45pm, Sat 10am–4.30pm, Sun 12pm–4pm.*

HANNE ANDERSEN JEWELLERY
1st Floor, Capital on the Quay, 226 Lambton Quay, tel 471-2814, www.hanne.co.nz
Established in 1988, Hanne Andersen specialises in designer jewellery in silver, gold and platinum, created by New Zealand artists. A good range of paua, greenstone and gemstones. *Open Mon–Thurs 9am–5.30pm, Fri 9am–7pm, Sat 10am–4pm, Sun 11am–4pm.*

JEWELLERY ARTS STUDIO
Cable Car Lane, Lambton Quay, tel 472-8866, www.jewelleryartsstudio.co.nz
Contemporary New Zealand jewellery designed and made on site plus work by other well-known jewellery artists from around the country. *Open Mon–Thurs 9am–5.30pm, Fri 9am–7pm, Sat/Sun 10am–4pm (open Sundays in summer.*

Feel Like Fashion Ships?

The *Inconstant* was a 600-tonne Canadian sailing vessel that hit rocks entering Wellington harbour a few years after it was built in 1848. The damaged ship was sold to local businessman John Plimmer, who beached it at what is now Lambton Quay and used it as a warehouse. Its fore and aft sections were cut off and a roof added, giving it the appearance of an ark. Following the 1855 earthquake and subsequent land reclamation, the ark became landlocked, with only its superstructure poking out. In 1882 that structure was demolished and the remains buried by the building of the Bank of New Zealand. Pan forward over 100 years ... in 1997 the remains of 'Plimmer's Ark' were discovered under the building. Most of the remains were removed for preservation and storage, but you can see the bow on permanent display in the **Old Bank Shopping Arcade**.

In the middle of the arcade is an animated, musical clock that retells the arcade's history every hour, on the hour (three minutes long). The clock, made by a local clock-maker, was unveiled at the arcade's official opening in June 1999.

The *Old Bank Shopping Arcade* houses many designer fashion stores including **Andrea Moore, Ricochet, Nicolas Blanchet, Ruby, Stella Gregg** and **Satori**. One of the highlights is the award-winning **Rixon Groove** – shirts, ties and accessories, plus perfect fit made-to-measure, and BYO fabric – a Wellington favourite. And don't miss **Workshop**.

Old Bank Shopping Arcade, corner Lambton Quay & Customhouse Quay, www.oldbank.co.nz. *Open Mon–Thurs 9am–6pm, Fri 9am–7pm, Sat 10am–4pm, Sun 11am–3pm.*

MINNIE COOPER

29 Hunter Street, tel 473-7946

Minnie Cooper is part of the Old Bank Shopping Arcade, but its entrance is on Hunter Street. This is a terrific little shop selling footwear, bags and knits for girls going places. All stylish and functional, all designed and made in New Zealand, and as popular as ever with Wellington ladies after 12 years of excellent service. *Open Mon–Fri 9.30am–6pm, Sat 10am–4pm, Sun 11am–3pm.*

HOUSE OF HANK
145 Willis Street, tel 381-0209, www.houseofhank.com
Hank Cubitt – friend of many and tailor to the stars. Hank crafts
innovative and unique menswear in fantastic cloth and colour, for
those who want their individuality to shine through. From business
shirts with a twist to extravagant eveningwear to funky casuals,
House of Hank has something for every man. Made-to-measure,
perfect fit and unique. *Open Mon–Fri 9am–6pm, Sat 10.30am–3.30pm.*

STARFISH
128 Willis Street, tel 385-3722, www.starfish.co.nz
Wellington-designed, New Zealand-made women's and men's
clothing with a loyal following. Designers Laurie Foon and Carleen
Schollum create original clothing that reflects, they say, the New
Zealand lifestyle and environment. Also stocks New Zealand labels
Commence, DNA, Insidious Fix, Adam Gibbs, Angeline Harrington,
Patrick James, NotApplicable, Sabatini and Thunderlily. *Open Mon–
Thurs 9.30am–6pm, Fri 9.30am–8pm, Sat 10am–5pm, Sun 11am–4pm.*

VOON
142 Willis Street, tel 801-8292, www.voon.co.nz
As a young girl, Sophie Voon liked to design clothes for her dolls.
Twenty or so years later she is still making clothes, but now for
grown-ups. More likely to be influenced by history and art rather
than fashion fads, Sophie is known for her use of beautiful fabric
and quirky detailing in a range of dresses, skirts, tops and shirts. Go
here for reasonably priced designer fashion and cool accessories too.
A favourite. *Open Mon–Thurs 10am–6pm, Fri 10am–8pm, Sat 10am–4pm, Sun
11.30am–4pm.*

JUNO
Shop 8, 142 Willis Street, tel 384-5557, www.fashionnz.co.nz/juno
Juno began as a vintage clothing store located in Wellington's
red light district. Four years ago designer/owner Rebekah Greig
launched the shop's own house label, which quickly found favour
with city women and abroad. Alterations service and personal
consultations by appointment too. *Open Mon–Thurs 10am–6pm, Fri 10am–
7pm, Sat 10am–4pm.*

SHOPPING

QUOIL CONTEMPORARY JEWELLERY
149 Willis Street, tel 384-1499
Representing around 30 New Zealand jewellers, Quoil regularly
holds exhibitions by both established and emerging artists and
was the first contemporary jewellery gallery in Wellington to
incorporate a workshop into the retail/exhibition space. It's known
for its diverse collections, knowledgeable staff and its support of
jewellery making. *Open Mon–Thurs 10am–6pm, Fri 10am–7pm, Sat 11am–3pm.*

ROBYN MATHIESON
89 Victoria Street, tel 499-0409, www.fashionnz/robynmathieson
A Wellington-based label going for more than 12 years. Simple,
stylish clothing made from quality fabric. The emphasis is on
comfort and cut, workable styles for the modern professional.
Mainly womenswear, with some menswear and babywear. *Open Mon–
Thurs 10am–6pm, Fri 10am–8pm, Sat 10am–4.30pm, Sun 12pm–4pm.*

WORLD
98 Victoria Street, tel 472-1595, www.worldbrand.co.nz
Certainly one of the more internationally publicised New Zealand
fashion labels, designer Denise L'Strange-Corbet's unusual, avant-
garde garments will appeal to those who love to stand out, although
there's plenty of intelligently tailored hard-wearing classics too.
Colourful accessories. *Open Mon–Thurs 9.30am–6pm, Fri 9.30am–8pm, Sat
10am–5pm, Sun 12pm–4pm.*

KAREN WALKER
126 Wakefield Street, tel 499-3558, www.karenwalker.com
As worn by Madonna and Kelly Osborne. A 'concept-inspired fashion
design store, top-end-of-the-market, international, signature
clothing label', from casual to formal wear. *Open Mon–Thurs 10am–6pm,
Fri 10am–8pm, Sat 10am–5pm, Sun 11am–4pm.*

THE LAST FOOTWEAR COMPANY
41 Cuba Street, tel 473-3808
Stockist of its own-brand New Zealand-designed, handmade leather
shoes, belts and bags of quality craftsmanship, specialising in boots.
Also stocks Birkenstock, G&L Brothers, Konev and Wild South. *Open
Mon–Thurs 10am–6pm, Fri 10am–8pm, Sat 10am–4pm, Sun 12pm–3pm.*

MANDATORY
108 Cuba Street, tel 384-6107
An approachable and friendly men's boutique with a strong accent on modern classics and designer clothing. Contemporary corporate, urban fashion and clubwear. *Open Mon–Thurs 10.30am–6pm, Fri 10.30am–7.30pm, Sat 10.30am–4pm, Sun 12pm–4pm.*

AREA 51
Corner Cuba & Dixon Streets, tel 385-6590
Denim/street-style clothing for men and women. Stockists of New Zealand labels Huffer, Little Brother and Blanchet. We like their fabulous array of interesting shirts and consistently good service. *Open Mon–Thur 9am–5.30pm, Fri 9am–8pm, Sat 10am–5pm, Sun 10.30am–4pm.*

GOLD ORE SILVER MINE
Cuba Mall Left Bank, tel 801-7019
A manufacturing jeweller offering a large range of own-design greenstone, paua shell and coloured gemstone jewellery. *Open Mon–Thurs 8am–5.30pm, Fri 8am–7pm, Sat 9am–4pm.*

LAZULE
151 Cuba Street, tel 385-8418, www.lazule.co.nz
Lazule specialises in sterling silver jewellery and has a large range of paua shell, greenstone and semi-precious stones, for men and women of all ages. *Open Mon–Thurs 10am–5.30pm, Fri 10am–6pm, Sat 10am–4.30pm, Sun 11am–3pm.*

ZIGGURAT
144 Cuba Street, tel 385-1077
A popular fashion exchange that's been around for ages, specialising in designer labels, vintage and unique clothing and accessories, for men and women. Inexpensive, expressive clothing. Buy and sell. *Open Mon–Thurs 10am–6pm, Fri 10am–7pm, Sat 10am–5pm, Sun 11.30am–4pm.*

CARLY HARRIS
154 Cuba Street, tel 384-1863
An eclectic, colourful range of feminine designs made from unique eastern fabrics. Clothes in which to stand out. *Open Mon–Thurs 11am–6pm, Fri 11am–7pm, Sat 10am–5pm, Sun 11am–4pm.*

SHOPPING

HUNTERS AND COLLECTORS
219 Cuba Street, tel 384-8948
'Home of good old leather.' New and used vintage, modern, skate, street and punk clothing, footwear, leather and accessories. A Cuba Street landmark. Buy–sell–trade. *Open Mon–Thurs 10am–6pm, Fri 10am–8pm, Sat 10am–6pm.*

TEMPEST
160 Cuba Street, tel 384-4904
Elegant, classic, comfortable womenswear, all locally designed and made. *Open Mon–Thurs 10.30am–5.30pm, Fri 10.30am–6pm, Sat 10.30am–5pm, Sun 12pm–4.30pm.*

FRUTTI
176 Cuba Street, tel 384-6965
For a colourful selection of quirky clothing and accessories, Frutti is a must visit. The packed racks contain mostly womenswear, the majority made in Wellington, some of it one-off pieces and others made using vintage fabrics. Go there for fashion you won't find anywhere else. *Open Mon–Fri 10.30am–6pm, Sat 10am–6pm, Sun 11am–5pm.*

RECREATION
96 Aro Street, Aro Valley, tel 384-9896, mob 021-310903
Janet Dunn specialises in carefully crafting cast-off and retro fabrics into exciting and unique new fashion garments. Made-to-measure, or choose off-the-rack at her studio/boutique. Alterations and BYO fabric okay too. Zero-waste, wearable art, for those who like something different and affordable. One of many good reasons to walk up Aro Street. *Open Tues–Sun 11am–6pm, or by appointment.*

Hunting & Collecting, Cuba Street
Positively Wellington Tourism (Nick Servian)

If you're in *Thorndon*, you'll find *Labels* and *Secondo*, both dealing in secondhand designer clothing, and *Fiorella*, beautiful handmade gemstone and pearl jewellery.

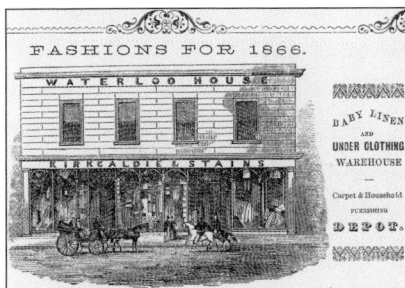

FASHIONS FOR 1866.

WATERLOO HOUSE

KIRKCALDIE & STAINS

BABY LINEN
AND
UNDER CLOTHING
WAREHOUSE

Carpet & Household
FURNISHING
DEPOT.

Kirkcaldie & Stains is one of New Zealand's oldest businesses.

Scottish-born John Kirkcaldie and Englishman Robert Stains established their first store in a shed on the beach at Port Nicholson in November 1863. Two years later, Wellington had become the capital of the colony and the store had moved into new premises, advertising the latest novelties from London and Paris in the *Evening Post*. Their business moved to its present site on Lambton Quay and grew, its prosperity matching that of the city.

After 1886, when Robert Stains returned to England, John Kirkcaldie and his sons headed the business in Wellington – and for a time also in Napier.

At the beginning of the depression in the 1930s financial difficulties forced the Kirkcaldie family to sell the business to British Overseas Stores. There followed 50 years of British control, until the store was returned to New Zealand ownership in 1984.

During its long history Kirkcaldie & Stains has survived many upheavals, earthquakes, fire and flood, and a major building reconstruction in the late 1980s. But through all the changes the store has continued the tradition of John Kirkcaldie and Robert Stains in providing for 'The Ladies of Wellington and Public generally in Town and Country'. That's us.

'Kirks', as we call it, is a classic department store offering a refined shopping experience in an elegant and ambient environment. This 'sole survivor of the capital's department stores is the pride of its citizens and a magnet for tourist shoppers' (says *The Merchant*).

Open Mon–Thurs 9am–5.30pm, Fri 9am–7pm, Sat 10am–4pm, Sun 11am–4pm.

Books and Music

For children's bookshops, see CHILDREN AND PARENTS.

MILLWOOD GALLERY
291b Tinakori Road, Thorndon, tel 473-5178
Tucked away in Thorndon's historic Tinakori village, Millwood Gallery is a combination of bookstore and art gallery. Here you'll find a beautiful and well-selected range of books, cards and gift-wrap plus original paintings and prints by contemporary New Zealand artists; the gallery also specialises in Wellington images. *Open Mon–Fri 9am–5.30pm, Sat 10am–4pm, Sun (Dec only) 12pm–4pm.*

BENNETTS GOVERNMENT BOOKSHOP
Corner Bowen Street & Lambton Quay, tel 499-3433
Interested in government legislation? Law? Politics? This shop's for you. Bennetts also has an excellent New Zealand section, plus plenty of popular fiction and non-fiction from around the world. *Open Mon–Thurs 8am–6pm, Fri 8am–7pm, Sat 10am–2pm.*

PARSONS BOOKS AND MUSIC
126 Lambton Quay, tel 472-4587
'Wellington's oldest independent, by a nose.' Founded in the 1950s by bookselling legend Roy Parsons, this Lambton Quay landmark remains family owned and operated. Parsons stocks more than 15,000 classical music CDs, videos and DVDs, as well as all sorts of books. A retro shop harking back to a more romantic retailing era. Coffee shop too. *Open Mon–Thurs 9am–5.30pm, Fri 9am–6pm, Sat 10am–4pm.*

CAPITAL BOOKS
23 Waring Taylor Street, tel 473–9358
The city's best range of technical books – computing, business, crafts, hobbies, etc. Family business. *Open Mon–Thurs 8.30am–5.30pm, Fri 8.30am–7.30pm, Sat 10am–4pm, Sun 12pm–4pm.*

CD STORE
250 Lambton Quay, tel 471–1188
An extensive range of CDs and DVDs, and over 25 listening stations. Import service for those hard to find titles. Child-friendly café. *Open Mon–Thurs 8am–7pm, Fri 7am–8pm, Sat 9am–6pm, Sun 10am–4pm.*

DYMOCKS
360–366 Lambton Quay, tel 472-2080, www.dymocks.co.nz
A popular bookshop in the middle of town. According to the *Lord of the Rings Location Guide*, Dymocks stocks 'the largest range of Tolkien books in New Zealand', and it's got the Tolkien collectable figures too. There's a carefully selected range of New Zealand books, postcards, posters and stationery, with overseas wrap, pack and post available. Worldwide book search. Winner of numerous nationwide bookshop awards including 'Group Bookseller of the Year' four years running. *Open Mon–Thurs 9am–6pm, Fri 9am–8pm, Sat 9am–5pm, Sun 10am–4pm.*

WHITCOULLS
The biggest Wellington branch of this nationwide chain is at 312 Lambton Quay – three floors of stationery, calendars and books of every kind including a good children's section on the 1st floor. There are several other branches around the city including Cuba Street and Courtenay Place. *Open Mon–Thurs 8am–6pm, Fri 8am–9pm, Sat 9am–6pm, Sun 10am–4pm.*

UNITY BOOKS
57 Willis Street, tel 499-4245/0800-4-UNITY, email unity.books@clear.net.nz
A stockholding bookshop committed to New Zealand publishing and fast access to international imports. Strong on fiction, history, politics and cookery. Review board, staff recommendations, special orders. *Open Mon–Thurs 9am–6pm, Fri 9am–7pm, Sat 10am–4pm, Sun 11am–4pm.*

FIRM RECORDS
Shop 6, 120 Victoria Street, tel 381-3074, www.firmrecords.co.nz, FM 107
Underground vinyl pimps. Dance ticket outlet. Supporting Wellington's DJ community, upfront shipments weekly. *Open Mon–Fri 11.30am–6pm, Sat 11.30am–4.30pm.*

PINNACLE BOOKS
142 Willis Street, tel 384-4563, www.pinaclebooks.co.nz
A specialist bookstore focused on spirituality, health, bodywork, psychology, counselling, the occult and astrology. Pinnacle also stocks a large range of tarot cards, CDs and tapes. Worldwide book search. *Open Mon–Thurs 9am–6pm, Fri 9am–8pm, Sat 10am–4pm.*

SHOPPING

FISH EYE DISCS

James Smiths Corner, Manners Street, tel 473-4088, www.fisheyediscs.co.nz
Delectable CDs for the discerning and curious. Friendly, knowledgeable staff always ready with a spot-on recommendation. Go here for personal service. *Open daily 9am–6pm.*

SLOW BOAT RECORDS

183 Cuba Street, tel 385-1330
The oldest music shop in Wellington. New and secondhand CDs and records, tapes, videos and DVDs. Imported vinyl and CDs. Buy, sell and trade around the world with, allegedly, 'a number of more famous pop stars amongst our customers'. *Open Mon–Thurs 9.30am–6pm, Fri 9.30am–8pm, Sat 10am–5pm, Sun 11am–5pm.*

REAL GROOVY

Corner Cuba & Abel Smith Streets, tel 385-2020, www.realgroovy.co.nz
A wide range of new and secondhand music, movies and games. Trade-ins welcome. Satisfying browsing in all areas. *Open Mon–Sun 9am–6pm, late night Fri until 9pm.*

DMC

78-86 Manners Mall, tel 385-8602, www.dmcworld.co.nz
DJ equipment and accessories. Clued-up, friendly staff make for informative and pleasurable browsing and chatter about the latest technology & tunes. *Open Mon-Thurs 10am-6pm, Fri 10am-7pm, Sat 10am-5pm.*

Secondhand Bookshops, buy–sell–exchange

Quilters, 110 Lambton Quay – rare books, New Zealand history and literature a speciality

Ferret, 123 Cuba Street – 'poke your nose in' and see for yourself

Bellamy's, 105 Cuba Street – wide range; sheet music

Bizy Bee's, corner Manners & Cuba Streets – wide range; all genres

Arty Bee's, 17 Courtenay Place – sistershop to Bizy Bee's; all genres

Recycled Book Warehouse, 16 Taine Street, Taita – wide range, strong on cookery and science fiction

Archway Books, SH1, Pukerua Bay – New Zealand collectable books

Antiques and Collectables

The Wellington antiques and collectables market is active with plenty of browsing to be found in the city and beyond.

A handful of shops close together in the *city centre* make for an easy excursion on foot:

Memory Lane, 40 Ghuznee Street – antiques, curious, collectables

Ascot Traders, 166 Cuba Street – antiques, collectables, bric-a-brac

David N White Gallery, 88 Abel Smith Street – antiques, curios and collectables

Sign of the Times, 311 Willis Street – retro furniture, fabric, fittings and ornaments

Offbeat Originals, Shop 6, Left Bank, Cuba Mall – kitsch

Antiques Centre, 60 Vivian Street – antique furniture, china, silver

AA Traders, Wakefield Market – antiques, curios and collectables

If you're interested in musical instruments visit **Alistair's Music**, 225 Cuba Street, (mainly strings including banjos, some woodwind).

Thorndon has several good antique shops:

Pleasant Place Antiques, 356 Tinakori Road – china, jewellery, silver, glass, furniture, tools

Cherry Orchard Antiques, 344 Tinakori Road – jewellery, silver & gold, porcelain, glass, paintings, furniture

Tinakori Antiques, 291a Tinakori Road – jewellery, porcelain, glass, paintings, furniture

Shamrock Antiques, 228 Tinakori Road – furniture, silver and plate, crystal and glass, ceramics

Don Macinnes Antiques, 157 Thorndon Quay – fine furniture

Antiquodeco, 83 Old Hutt Road – china, glass and deco

In **Kelburn**, **Peter Wedde Antiques**, 86 Upland Road, stocks Georgian and Regency period items.

Newtown's Adelaide Junction (intersection of Adelaide & Riddiford) makes an excellent stop for the secondhand shopper, just a short bus ride from Courtenay Place:

Adelaide Junction Antiques – china, furniture, toys, curios, crystal

Hobsons – collectables including New Zealand art and pottery

Riddiford Corner – antiques, curios, collectables and art deco

Ravens Nest – antiques, curios and collectables

Further up **Riddiford Street**, you'll find a favoured hunting ground for interesting and affordable 50s, 60s and 70s stuff. **Gawjus Fings** (132 Riddiford Street) stocks a fabulous array of furniture and decorative items. To quote the owners, 'you have to remember that what really inspired all this was the idea of going to the moon. Everything had sharp edges. American cars had wings, lounge suites had wings … a lot of it serves no purpose, it was made to be a piece of art.'

In **Kilbirnie**, visit **Owens Antiques** (51 Bay Road) for antiques, curios and collectables.

Jackson Street, Petone offers satisfying antique shopping, with a wide range of goods on offer, but particularly strong on furniture. Try **Duveen** (121 Jackson Street), **Colonial Curios** (165), **Ladybird** (185), **Margie's Bazaar** (190), **Two Four Seven** (247), **Soucheby's** (328) and **Charlotte's Web** (376).

The Passing Show in **Tawa** (68 Main Road) stocks Georgian, Regency and Victorian furniture, artwork, clocks and other collectables, as well as a huge range of dining chairs.

Dunbar Sloane auctioneers hold 'investment and affordable' art auctions three times a year (7 Maginnity Street, www.dunbarsloane.com). Visit its website for details.

Food and Wine

Need a bottle to BYO or something tasty for a summer picnic? We recommend you see what's on offer at Wellington's specialist food and wine merchants. If it's *wholefoods* and *organics* you're after, see WELL-BEING AND BODY BEAUTIFUL.

BORDEAUX BAKERY
220 Thorndon Quay, tel 499-8334
The lover of true French patisserie cannot go past Bordeaux. Real-live French bakers make mouth-watering traditional breads and cakes. Local food critic Des Britten voted Bordeaux best bakery two years running. Brasserie menu too. Plenty of room for children. *Open Sun–Mon 7.30am–3pm, Tues–Sat 7.30am–4pm.*

RUMBLES
32 Waring Taylor Street, tel 472-7045, www.rumbleswine.co.nz
A haven of hedonism at the suity end of the city, Rumbles professes to offer 'perhaps' the widest range of imported wines in New Zealand. It's hard to argue: this is an impressive selection and, when you've been in the business for 20 years, you're obviously doing something right. The Kiwi wine range is relatively small but rigorously selected. Also stocked are unusual beers, spirits and liqueurs. *Open Mon–Thurs 9am–7pm, Fri 9am–8pm, Sat 10am–5pm.*

DE SPA CHOCOLATIER
Old Bank Arcade, 233 Lambton Quay, tel 922-0613, www.despa.co.nz
Handmade Belgian chocolates by patisserie chef and chocolatier, Monsieur Jean-Marie, who has more than 30 years' experience including purveying to the Belgian royal family. Choose from more than 75 varieties, including sugar- and dairy-free. Elegant gift boxes. *Open Mon–Thurs 9am–6pm, Fri 9am–7pm, Sat 10am–4pm, Sun 11am–4pm.*

BOND WINES AND SPIRITS
8 Bond Street, tel 473-0228
A small independent wine merchant specialising in New Zealand and imported wine, beer and spirits. Knowledgable, enthusiastic staff (with the 'Bond girls' in charge). National and international delivery. *Open Mon–Thurs 10am–7pm, Fri 10am–8pm, Sat 11.30am–4.30pm.*

SHOPPING

DIXON STREET DELI
45 Dixon Street, tel 384-2436
A long established Wellington foodies' landmark, Dixon Street Deli is known for its worldly goods – continental cheese and small goods, oils and vinegars, and fine bittersweet chocolate. They serve café-style food and fresh juice alongside. Watch the world go past the window. *Open Mon–Fri 7.30am–5pm, Sat 8.30am–4pm.*

THE NUT STORE
229 Cuba Street, tel 801-5645
A quirky little shop serving a niche market, The Nut Store specialises in New Zealand-grown, organic nuts and nut products. They also stock spices, dried fruit and preserves. Enjoy toasty nuts from their warmer on a chilly day. National and international mail order available. *Open Mon–Fri 10am–5pm, Sat 10.30am–2pm (open later in summer).*

WELLINGTON TRAWLING SEAMARKET
220 Cuba Street, tel 384-8461
Fish processor, exporter and importer, so it's fresh, and there's plenty of it. Fresh fillets, shellfish, whitebait, caviar, fresh and smoked salmon. Good fish & chips too. Off-street parking. *Open (for fresh fish) Mon–Thurs 7am–7pm, Fri 7am–7pm, Sat 7am–7pm, Sun 8am–7pm.*

PANDORO PANETTERIA
2 Allen Street, tel 385-4478
This fine bakery can be found at both ends of Wellington, one in Woodward Street, the other in Allen. Pandoro bakes an exhaustive range of breads, cakes and other goods. It prides itself on its use of natural ingredients, using no artificial flavourings or preservatives and is free from genetically modified ingredients. *Open Mon–Fri 7am–6pm, Sat/Sun 7am–4pm.*

MR CHAN'S
100 Cable Street, tel 384-6622
Mr Chan's is Wellington's biggest Asian supermarket and stocks a wide variety of groceries, exotic spices from India, Thailand, China, Japan and Korea, as well as fresh produce. Oriental kitchenware also on sale including woks, chopsticks and sushi sets. *Open Mon–Wed 8.30am–7.30pm, Thurs–Fri 8.30am–8pm, Sat 8.30am–7.30pm, Sun 8.30am–6.30pm.*

MOORE WILSON FRESH MARKET

Corner Tory & College Streets, tel 384-9906

The mecca for Wellington home cooks, Moore Wilson's fabulous food includes meat and fish, fresh produce, bread and arguably the best cheese counter in town. Stockists of many of New Zealand's finest foods, and some imported treats. Perfect for picnic provisions or a one-stop dinner-party shop. *Open Mon–Sat 7.30am–7pm, Sun 9am–6pm.*

BROOKLYN BREAD AND BAGELS

29 College Street, tel 802-4111

'At night we bake lots of bagels …' During the day, the bakery sells them alongside good food and coffee. The Brooklyn bagel bakers were the first in New Zealand to bake a bagel; now they bake lots of other breads too. *Open daily 7.30am–4pm.*

TRUFFLE FOOD AND WINE

12 College Street, tel 385-2802, www.truffle.net.nz

'A slice of Europe in the capital.' Everyday European products such as rice, olive oils, mustards and pasta, and indulgences like real truffles, Iranian saffron, duck confit and Burgundian snails. Tastings available, and expert help on hand. The wine showroom has mostly Italian, Spanish and French wines in all price ranges. More than 400 aged wines spanning the last 20 years. Wine tastings on Saturdays. *Open Mon–Fri 10am–6pm, Sat 10am–4pm.*

REGIONAL WINES AND SPIRITS

15 Ellice Street (Basin Reserve), tel 385-6952, www.regionalwines.co.nz

Absolutely excellent. This large shop stocks more than 4000 wines, 250 single malts and Wellington's best range of imported and Kiwi beers (some fill your own flagon). Prepare to be dazzled. Knowledgable, affable staff. Tasting events. *Open Mon–Sat 9am–10pm, Sun 10am–6.30pm.*

LE MOULIN

248 Willis Street, tel 382-8118

This tiny bakery produces absolutely delicious patisserie, crispy baguettes and traditional Kiwi pies. Their almond tarts are a knockout. Without a doubt, deserving of its loyal local following. *Open Tues–Thurs 7.30am–5pm, Fri 7.30am–5pm, Sat/Sun 8am–2pm.*

AROBAKE

83 Aro Street, Aro Valley, tel 384-5473

Once the haven of students and bohemians, the increasingly sophisticated Aro Valley is home to probably the finest custard square in New Zealand. Established in 1989, Arobake has dedicated itself to producing quality goods from artisan breads to European biscuits and confectionary. Influenced by traditional Swiss baking, natural methods and ingredients are used to create excellent breads and patisserie. Good pies too. Eat in with fine coffee. Yum. *Open Mon–Fri 7am–5.15pm, Sat 7am–3.30pm.*

HORSERADISH DELICATESSEN

90 Upland Road, Kelburn, tel 475-3784

A top-notch local deli. Homemade pies and quiches, muffins, cakes and cookies. Perfect for that Botanic Garden picnic. Also stocks fresh bread, deli meats, dried goods, preserves and award-winning olive oil. Some gluten- and wheat-free products. *Open Mon–Fri 8am–6pm, Sat 9am–2pm.*

KALAMATA DELICATESSAN

4 Gipps Street, Karori, tel 476-4741

The best foodie pitstop in Karori and a popular local meeting place, Kalamata is a happy mixture of big city café, surburban delicatessan and small-town tearoom. It stocks a carefully selected range of specialist food and confectionery for the pick-up-and-go customer, as well as home-cooked café fare for the sit-downs. It's all very good, and as for those sweet slices...! *Open Mon–Fri 7am–4.30pm, Sat 7am–2.30pm.*

GIPPS STREET BUTCHERY

8 Gipps Street, Karori, tel 476-9584

Next door to Kalamata is a proper New Zealand butchery with a fine reputation for high quality meats and personal service. Gipps Street Butchery specialises in homemade bacon and ham traditionally cured using Murrellen stress-free pork from Canterbury. Butcher Bill Allen has also been making South African boerwors sausages for 25 years, satisfying sausage lovers all over town. *Open Mon–Fri 7am–6.15pm, Sat 7am–2pm.*

SHOPPING

MEDITERRANEAN FOOD WAREHOUSE

42 Constable Street, Newtown, tel 939-8100, www.medifoods.co.nz

Antonio Cuccurullo, like many southern Italian immigrants settling in Wellington in the 1950s, found himself living and working in the fisheries, strongly rooted in Island Bay. He ran Wellington Fisheries in Cuba Street for 42 years with partner Camillo Amitrano until his sons took over the business in 1990. Gino and Joe, recognising a gap in the market, began importing the foods they had grown up with – pasta, olives, olive oils and tomato products. Today their popular Newtown shop stocks every imaginable item – our own Little Italy. Good wood-fired pizza café on site, cooking classes and online shopping too. *Open Mon–Fri 8am–6pm, Sat 8am–4pm.*

WELLINGTON HALAL MEAT

155a Riddiford Street, Newtown, tel 380-0900

'I don't want to be a millionaire, so I ask a fair price.' Well, you can't argue with that. Mr Khan sells all sorts of halal meats including goat and handmade sausages. *Open Mon–Wed 8am–6pm, Thurs/Fri 8am–7pm, Sat 9am–5pm, Sun 10am–3pm.*

ISLAND BAY BUTCHERY

127 The Parade, Island Bay, tel 383-7066

Super sausages from an award-winning butchery. Old English and Cumberland, Spanish chorizo, Greek loukanika, German bratwurst, various Italian and venison sausages too. Many more, all delicious. Other small goods (such as salami and black pudding) and high quality cuts available. Well worth the journey. *Open Mon–Fri 7am–6.30pm, Sat 8am–2pm.*

LA BELLA ITALIA

10 Nevis Street, Petone, tel 566-9303, www.labellaitalia.co.nz

Authenic Italian delicacies direct from Italy including prosciutto, cheese, anchovies, olive oils, beer, wine and limoncello. Owner Antonio Cacace is freshly imported himself, coming from Massa Lubrense where his grandfather founded a salumeria (cured meat shop) in the early 1900s, so his credentials are good. Cooking classes. *Open Mon–Fri 7.30am–5pm, Sat 9am–5pm, Sun 10am–5pm.*

Local Delicacies and Delights

You'll find the following products in outlets all over town, but your best hit rate will be at *Moore Wilson Fresh*, College Street.

Cheese lovers! Try **Zany Zeus** – local lad gets Greek–Cypriot mum to show him the cheese-making ropes, and away he goes! Michael Matsis' award-winning cheeses include halloumi (the house speciality), along with feta, ricotta and mozarella. Also readily available around town is the popular **Kapiti** range (they do ice cream too – try fig and honey). The Wairarapa produces the delightful **Saratoga** chevre and **Kingsmeade** range.

Sweet-tooths must try **Loukoumi** Turkish delight – the Palamidas' family recipe handed down from generation to generation, the fruits available to us fresh. Flavours include rose, raspberry, vanilla and almond. **Chocolate Temptations by Aida**, available from *Dorothy's* on Cuba Street, include truffles and fondant fillings (some sugar-free), made by a master from best-quality European chocolate. **Wakelin House** of Masterton fashion fine fudge and panforte.

Harrington's Small Goods produce naturally cured sausages, bacon and the like, made the traditional way with New Zealand-only meats, while **Bells Continental Smallgoods** make award-winning bratwurst and kransky. **Francois**, the very French, very popular Thorndon bistro, packs a perfect paté.

Beer drinkers should look out for **Katipo,** whose brews include pale ale, strong ale and stout – all highly regarded by the experts. You'll find them at the *Parrot & Jigger* (499 Hutt Road, Lower Hutt) or by the flagon from *Regional Wines & Spirits*. It's also on tap at *Bodega*, as is Kapiti's **Tuatara** range. The **Wellington Brewing Company,** (4 Taranaki Street), is brewing several styles on site; their Sassy Red and Wicked Blonde are medal winners.

THE DUTCH SHOP
89 Jackson Street, Petone, tel 568-9338
The only Dutch shop in Wellington. Stocks various cheeses, smoked sausages and eel, sauerkraut, all manner of other Dutch products, as well as souvenirs. *Open Mon–Sat 9am–5pm.*

Outdoor and Sports Equipment

MAINLY TRAMPING

39 Mercer Street, tel 473-5353

Going tramping/hiking/walking in the bush/forest/woods? Go here. 'Happy, switched-on staff that tell me what I need to know, quickly.' A comprehensive range of outdoor equipment including many New Zealand brands. *Open Mon–Thurs 9am–5.30pm, Fri 9am–7pm, Sat 10am–4pm.*

TISDALLS OUTDOORS

52 Willis Street, tel 472-0485, www.tisdalls.co.nz

Tramping, adventure, travel and fishing tackle, since 1889. Still family owned, Tisdalls stocks a range of New Zealand-made and imported equipment including reputable brands of sleeping bag, backpack and boot. Fly and salt fishing tackle. Loads of gadgets. Overall winner of the Wellington 'Top Shop' award in 2002. *Open Mon–Fri 9am–5.30pm, Sat 10am–4pm, Sun 11am–3pm.*

STIRLING SPORTS

44 Willis Street, tel 472-8108

'We love our sport,' they say. Stirling Sports is a one-stop shop for sports lovers, from dart and pool players, to those lively enough to pick up a racquet or even chase a ball! If you need it, you'll probably find it here. Loads of All Blacks apparel too, for the armchair sportsmen, of course! (Sorry. Ed.) *Open Mon–Fri 9am–6pm, Sat 10am–5pm, Sun 11am–4pm.*

STEVE'S FISHING SHOP

49 Ghuznee Street, tel 384-5105

Steve Reed has been fishing around Wellington for more than 35 years, and his shop (established in 1985) is Wellington's only specialist fishing store. It stocks a wide range of saltwater rods, reels, accessories and bait, and offers a prompt rod and reel repair service. The shop looks like Neptune's cave with its impressive display of fish mounts (marlin, tuna, kingfish and the very large mako shark) and antique tackle. *Open Mon–Thurs 9am–5.30pm, Fri 9am–7pm, Sat 9.30am–3pm.*

CHEAPSKATES
60 Cuba Street, tel 499-0455
Serving the skating community for well over a decade.
Skateboards, inline skates, parts and accessories, lots of clothing
and footwear for all. *Open Mon–Thurs 9am–6pm, Fri 9am–8pm, Sat 10am–*
5pm, Sun 11am–4pm.

BOARDROOM
37 Taranaki Street, tel 382-9382
The oldest skateboard and snowboard shop in town, established in
1989. Equipment, accessories, clothing and footwear. *Open Mon–Thurs*
9.30am–6pm, Fri 9.30am–8pm, Sat 10am–4pm, Sun 11am–4pm.

BURKES CYCLES
16-30 Coutts Street, Kilbirnie, tel 387-3036, www.burkescycles.co.nz
Wellington's best selection of cycles and accessories. Bikes for
children and grown-ups, and a solid selection of accessories and
clothing. Recently judged best New Zealand bike shop. Sales,
servicing and repairs available, plus try before you buy in the new
outdoor test area. Bike hire available. *Open Mon–Fri 8.30am–5.30pm*
(Thurs late night until 8pm), Sat/Sun 10am–4pm.

ON YER BIKE
Corner Ghuznee & Victoria Streets, tel 384-8480
A small bike shop run by 'guys who like riding bikes'. Cross-
country free ride and down-hill a speciality. Sales, repair and
servicing. A mix of bikes and a wide range of accessories and
top-end trick bits. *Open Mon–Thurs 8.30am–5.30pm, Fri 8.30am–8pm, Sat*
9am–4pm.

MUD CYCLES
1 Allington Road, Karori, tel 476-4961, www.mudcycles.co.nz
Makara Mountain Bike Park adventure specialist offering shop,
bike service, retail and rentals. Rental includes helmet, pump
and spare tube. Cost half day $25, full day $40, longer term rates
available as well as touring trailers, racks and panniers. City drop
off and collection. Lessons for riders of all levels. *Open Mon–Sun*
9am–6pm.

SURF N SNOW

45 Cuba Street, tel 473-3371

Surfing and snowboarding specialists offering a full range of boards and accessories, plus clothing for the mountain, beach or street. Full workshop and repair services. Rumoured to have taught the hobbits how to surf (now there's a claim to fame!). *Open Mon–Thurs 9am–6pm, Fri 9am–8.30pm, Sat 10am–5pm, Sun 11am–5pm.*

WILD WINDS

Chaffers Marina, Overseas Terminal, Oriental Bay, tel 384-1010, www.wildwinds.co.nz

Windsurfing, kitesurfing, snowboarding and surfing equipment, accesories and lessons. *Open Mon–Fri 10am–6pm, Sat 10am–3pm, Sun 11am–3pm.*

SWIM SHOP

132 Oriental Parade, tel 385-0362

New Zealand's largest range of swimwear including competition wear and gear for children. An extensive range of goggles, plus wetsuits, beachwear and other watersports accessories. Mailorder available. Situated next to Freyberg Pool and Oriental Bay beach. *Open Mon-Fri 9am–6pm, Sat/Sun 10am–5pm.*

THE REAL SURF COMPANY

Corner Kingsford Smith & Lyall Bay Parade, Lyall Bay, tel 387-8798

Specialising in custom surfboards, Real Surf also stocks a variety of branded boards, accessories and is local agent for Seventh Wave wetsuits. Board and wetsuit repairs. *Open daily 12pm–4pm (shorter hours in winter).*

THE GOLF WAREHOUSE

101 Waterloo Quay, tel 499-7754, www.golfdiscount.co.nz

New Zealand's largest golf retailer stocking a wide range of quality equipment including Calloway, Taylormade and Hippo. Test clubs on the driving range, and take advice from professional staff, all experienced golfers. Repair service. *Open Mon–Fri 9am–6.30pm, Sat/Sun 9am–5.30pm.*

SHOPPING

Children and Parents

Track down that emergency toy, cloth nappy or maternity bra ...

TIDDLEYPOM

140 Victoria Street, tel 384-8600, www.tiddleypom.co.nz
Wooden toys, science equipment, musical instruments, fairies, puppets, puzzles, books, art and craft material, and newborn baby toys. Well displayed for easy browsing, and staff are happy to offer suggestions if you run out of ideas. *Mindscapes* and *Modelcrafts & Hobbies* next door are also well worth a look. *Open Mon–Thurs 9am–5.30pm, Fri 9.30am–6.30pm, Sat 10am–4pm.*

THE PLAY GROUND

Capital E, Civic Square, tel 801–6987, www.theplayground.co.nz
A 'hands-on toy store' where children are actually encouraged to pull stuff off the shelves. Heaps of gorgeous toys to play with including books and art supplies plus many hard to find strategy games. Let 'em loose, and have a chat with the ever-patient Lynley and her helpful staff. *Open Mon–Sat 9.30am–5.30pm, Sun 10am–5pm.*

THE MET SHOP

5 Swan Lane (off Cuba Street), tel 384-7683
Silly, zany, fun toys and gifts that will intrigue and entertain. Games, puzzles and mindbenders, kites and wind socks, animal toys – plastic, stuffed, fluffy, wild, native New Zealand and blow-up. For the budding scientist, there's chemistry and experimental sets as well as weather items – thermometers, wind speed dials, rainfall monitors, magnifiers and barometers. Puppets, bath toys and bubble fun. Perfect for those with pocket money. *Open Mon–Thurs 9.30am–5pm, Fri 9.30pm–6pm, Sat 10am–5pm, Sun 10am–4pm.*

BEADZ UNLIMITED

Level 2, James Smiths Corner (Cuba & Manners), tel 470-7776, www.beadzunlimited.com
Make your own jewellery with the help of experts, choosing from a staggering array of beautiful beads. This is great fun, good value and a really neat place to take older children. Adults will love it too. *Open Mon–Thurs 10am–5pm, Fri 10am–8pm, Sat 10am–6pm, Sun 10am–5pm.*

TE PAPA'S TREASURE STORE
Te Papa, Cable Street, tel 381-7013
A toy shop with a New Zealand focus. Books, games, toys, puppets, babywear and children's clothing. Complete Buzzy Bee range in stock, as well as a good selection of books on Maori legends, native birds, insects and fish. Merino wool leggings and hats and locally made T-shirts. Rugby games and card cricket. For younger children there's lots of soft toys and puppets, including irresistable native birds. A good selection of cheap items for pocket-money spenders. *Open daily 9.30am–6pm (late night Thurs until 9pm).*

TOYWORLD
20-24 Ballance Street, tel 473-0226
A large toy shop with something for every member of the family from infants to adults. Barbie to Star Wars, collectables, Gameboy, family games, soft toys. All the famous brands and a huge selection of board games. Endless browsing. *Open Mon–Thurs 9am–5.30pm, Fri 9am–6.30pm, Sat 10am–5pm, Sun 10am–4pm.*

THE CHILDREN'S BOOKSHOP
Shop 25, Bay Court Mall, Kilbirnie, tel 387-3905
Widely regarded as the best children's bookshop in the city – a wonderful shop with parents in mind: excellent pushchair access, free parking and a play area. Worldwide book search. *Open Mon–Wed 9am–5.30pm, Thurs 9am–7pm, Fri 9am–5.30pm, Sat 9.30am–4pm.*

THE FARAWAY TREE
31 Dundas Street, Seatoun, tel 380-8904
Fairy paradise! From costumes, music boxes and story books through to posters, calendars and cards – there's nothing Dorothy doesn't have. Make sure you keep an eye out for her beautiful handcrafted fairies. A magical wonderland! *Open Mon–Fri 9am–5pm, Sat 9am–4pm, Sun 12pm–4pm.*

ISLAND BAY STATIONERS
151 The Parade, Island Bay, tel 383-7102
Yes, it says it's a stationer, but wait until you see inside! A treasure trove of children's books! *Open Mon–Fri 9am–5pm, Sat 9am–12.30pm.*

SHOPPING

A good one-stop shopping centre for parents and carers is the **Capital Gateway Centre** on Thorndon Quay with four good outlets that should cover all bases.

Rascal is a very stylish baby and child store, complete with hundreds of products from toys, books and newborn clothing, through to nursery products, bedding and furniture, all carefully chosen by experienced parents. **Blume Maternity Essentials**, Wellington's only maternity boutique, makes comfortable, colourful, practical clothing for expectant mums, size 8–24. **Pumpkin Patch** stocks own-brand clothing 0–12 years, along with furniture, bedding and maternity wear. **JK Kids Gear** also stocks its own-brand children's clothing for 0–12 years including some footwear. *All stores open Mon–Fri 9.30am–5.30pm, Sat/Sun 10am–4pm.*

HOPSCOTCH

155 Karori Road, Karori, tel 476-0348, www.educationalexperience.co.nz
Quality educational toys for preschoolers through to primary school children. Part of the nationwide Educational Experience toy stores throughout New Zealand. *Open Mon–Thurs 9am–5pm, Fri 9am–5.30pm, Sat 9.30pm–3.30pm.* Two doors down is **Marsden Books**, a popular bookshop with books for all children of all ages, open similar hours.

BABY STAR

84 Constable Street, Newtown, tel 939-2225
New/pre-loved/hire. Two floors of mother and child gear, including buggies, cots, highchairs and other vital equipment. Reusable nappies and other newborn necessities. Maternity clothing includes their own designs, as well as Cocoon and Egg. There's also a selective range of clothes and shoes for babies and children through to 10 years. *Open Mon–Wed 10am–4pm, Thurs/Fri 10am–5pm, Sat 9.30pm–4pm.*

GUBBS

107 Manners Street, tel 384-3037
A very good independent shoe shop stocking colourful and funky children's shoes. Gubb's also stocks ballet, jazz and tap shoes, plus a wide variety of women's shoes, boots and sandals at fair prices. *Open Mon–Thurs 9am–5.30pm, Fri 9am–7pm, Sat 10am–4pm, Sun 12pm–4pm.*

MERRY-GO-ROUND

Churchill Drive Shopping Centre, Crofton Downs, tel 939-8855

A good selection of toys including the Papo French figurines and fairy & knight's castles, Madeline dolls and Groovy Girl collection. 'Girlie girlie' corner has decorated jewellery boxes, bracelets, hair ties and cute handbags (baubles, sequins and feathers abound). Soft TY beanies, magic tricks, wooden toys, dress-ups, boys stuff, games, pocket money pickings and loads of other stuff. Newborn gifts and clothes for children under 2 years and essential wear to fit up to 14 years; Ozone swimwear; selective pre-loved clothes and shoes. *Open Mon–Wed 9am–5.30pm, Thurs–Fri 9am–6pm, Sat 10am–5pm.*

THE NAPPY STORE

4 Burgess Rd, Johnsonville, tel 461-6693, www.thenappystore.co.nz

Stocks a large range of cloth and disposable nappies including Kooshies washables and ultra absorbent Cosie disposables. Bulk purchase discounts and free nappy delivery service (conditions apply). Also stocks Egg maternity wear, plus an array of nursery products, equipment, accessories, toys and gifts. Brands including Touchwood Cots, Mountain Buggy and Safe & Sound car seats are all here. *Open Mon–Fri 9.30am–5pm, Sat 9.30am–5pm.*

SHOPPING

Keeping the Kids Happy

For *playgrounds*, turn to page 38.

A few options for *rainy day fun* can be found on page 77.

Turn to the *Feeding the Family* section (page 129) for child-friendly cafés and restaurants.

For central city *baby-change facilities*, try Kirkcaldie & Stains (Lambton Quay), the Central Library (Civic Square) and Farmers (Cuba Street).

Do you know about *www.kidsnewzealand.com*? It's a useful website covering Dunedin, Christchurch, Wellington and Auckland that has listings for parents on all sorts of things including special events, party entertainers and venues, dance, music and art classes, sports, childcare, support organisations and school holiday programmes.

Positively Wellington Tourism (Nick Servian)

Dining Out

Food lovers will find plenty of lip-smacking satisfaction in Wellington, with over 300 restaurants and cafés to choose from.

The hallmarks of good Wellington cuisine are the use of local produce, seasonality and innovation. Our influences are international, but you'll soon see the incredible impact our Asia-Pacific neighbours have had on our eating habits. So expect plenty of classic contemporary food, mixed in with all sorts of aroma and spice. Some call it 'fusion'; we're so used to it now, it doesn't need a name: it's just New Zealand cuisine, and will be best enjoyed with our world class wine and top Wellington coffee.

So prepare to indulge! But where? Well, there are far too many fantastic places to mention here. So we bring you those that perform consistently well, based on the feedback from more than 50 local foodies. Listings appear in random order in the city centre, followed by those out of town (most easily accessible by bus).

License status is indicated. Most restaurants are BYO – you may 'bring your own' bottle of wine, served to you for a small fee. Top-end restaurants are all fully licensed, with the odd one allowing BYO on occasion. Many welcome **children**, and a few will have highchairs.

You'll find more places to eat in PUBS, BARS AND LIVE MUSIC. Many bakeries and delicatessens offer dine-in facilities too, and these can be found in SHOPPING along with wine merchants.

DINING OUT

Capital Coffee

In Wellington you will find a vibrant café culture serving up some of the best espresso machine coffee in the world.

The classic Wellington coffees are the latte and the flat white. And while there's a brisk trade in takeaway coffees, the definitive coffee experience is best had sitting down, drinking from thick, pleasantly warm, tactile Italian crockery, with just the right amount of finely textured milk blended with a short strong shot or two of espresso. At its best, it will not be too big or too milky, and will have complex layers of coffee flavour giving way to a smooth, dark chocolate finish. This is coffee as cuisine, not fast food.

What's remarkable is that this intense coffee culture has taken hold and flourished in the tiny capital city of a nation of tea drinkers in the middle of the Pacific.

When the first wave of real cafés opened at the end of the 1980s, consumers embraced them with remarkable fervour. The city has long had many well-travelled urbane residents hungry for sophistication and the next new thing. But good coffee swiftly reached beyond that influential elite, and caffeine became the recreational drug of choice for the mainstream.

Today, when you ask a Wellingtonian about cafés, you'll find them pleasantly opinionated about where to find the best latte, which have the nicest food, and where the service and vibe hits the spot. Stroll a few blocks in the city and a chorus of competing coffee brands beckon from windows and espresso machines, tempting you to try another latte. Established cafés buzz with regulars observing the rituals of caffeine-fuelled conversation and the pleasures of the all-day breakfast. Tiny espresso bars squeeze into ridiculously cramped spaces, pumping out takeaways while their customers linger on the footpath.

The café culture is diverse and sophisticated. Unlike the multinational glitz that surrounds northern hemisphere coffee, there is a relaxed antipodean confidence and a sense of personal pride in the product here. It's Wellington coffee and it's good.

by Chris Dillon

Cafés

Most of the cafés below offer counter food as well as a brunch and lunch menu. In the evenings, many move up a notch to offer a more upmarket dining experience. Some are licensed; some are not; none are BYO. For a fix on the fly, look out for **Fuel**.

What's on the menu? These are the most popular coffees, although there are numerous variations, and of course the ubiquitous hot chocolate with marshmallows.

> *Latte* – single espresso with lots of hot milk, often arriving in a glass
> *Flat White* – double shot of espresso with less milk than a latte
> *Cappuccino* – single espresso shot with fine foamy steamed milk, and a sprinkle of chocolate or cinnamon on top
> *Long Black* – double espresso, usually on top of hot water, no milk
> *Short Black* – single or double shot espresso, no milk

CAFÉ L'AFFARE
27 College Street, tel 385-9748, www.laffare.co.nz
A truly great Wellington café. For a start there's the aroma. After that there's superb coffee, consistently good food, efficient service, interesting interior, alfresco dining, and it's child friendly. Highly recommended. Licensed. *Open Mon–Fri 7am–4.30pm, Sat 8am–4pm.*

MASI
49 Willis Street, tel 473-3558
Superb coffee and the best Caesar salad in town. Owner Silo Tabuakovei is an award-winning barista, and her ever-popular café is a testament to her high standards. All-day brunch is a specialty, and the menu changes weekly to include seasonal, local produce. A good range of counter food, prepared with care. Prime people-watching spot in the window, and outside seating. *Open Mon–Fri 7am–5.30pm, Sat 8.30am–4.30pm, Sun 9.30am–4pm.*

OLIVE CAFE
170 Cuba Street, tel 802-5266
'Fantastic counter selection – tasty and fresh,' says one regular. Local food critic Des Britten rated this best café in 2002, and you can see why. Besides delicious contemporary fare served in a pleasant

DINING OUT

space, Olive has a relaxed feel, attentive staff and an attractive courtyard. It's immensely appealing when the evening menu kicks in at 6pm – perfect for a meal with friends or romantic dinner for two. From steak to lentil salad, with fine desserts, and organic ingredients where possible. Overall, Olive shows excellent attention to detail. Licensed. *Open Mon 8am–5pm, Tues–Fri 8am–10pm, Sat 9.30am–10pm, Sun 9.30am–5pm.*

FIDELS

234 Cuba Street, tel 801-6868

Laid back and out of the way, Fidels does the best fry-up and veggie breakfast in town. Proper crispy bacon at last, and top hollandaise too. Wholesome counter food, vegan options, smoothies. Courtyards. Always slick and busy. Licensed. *Open Mon–Fri 7.30am–late, Sat/Sun 9am–late.*

MIDNIGHT ESPRESSO

178 Cuba Street, tel 384-7014

The original and still one of the best, more than 10 years later. In fact, many would say that sitting in the Midnight window with Havana coffee and cake is the quintessential Wellington café experience. Its gorgeously garnished counter food is hearty, tasty and certainly not overpriced. Juices, smoothies, teas and hot food also available. And Midnight will be open when everywhere else is closed. *Open Mon–Fri 8.30am–3am, Sat/Sun 9am–3am.*

DELUXE

10 Kent Terrace, tel 801-5455

Sistership to Midnight, the original Deluxe is as popular as ever for its fine coffee stocks and fresh homemade counter food – mainly vegetarian and vegan. It has stayed, as it started, quite bohemian in feel, and frequently changing artwork gives you something new to look at. Sit outside to watch the comings and goings at the Embassy. *Open Mon–Fri 7am–late, Sat/Sun 8am–late.*

NIKAU GALLERY CAFÉ

City Gallery Building, Civic Square, tel 801-4168

A bright and airy café next to the City Gallery, Nikau is popular for an upmarket lunch (some sweet counter food). A focused menu should please everyone, and features regional produce, organic where possible. The food is prepared with care, and the service is efficient. Interesting wines available by the glass. Licensed. *Open Mon–Fri 7am–4pm (dinner Fri 5pm–8pm), Sat 9am–4pm.*

ASTORIA
159 Lambton Quay, tel 473-8500
In a pleasant spot in the heart of Lambton Quay, the European-style Astoria opens out on to Midland Park where it courts lunchers and loungers, especially on a sunny day. Mediterranean flavours dominate the menu, and there are many wines available by the glass. Bijou counter food and coffee roasted daily on the premises. Licensed. *Open Mon–Fri 7am–7.30pm, Sat/Sun 9am–4pm.*

MALO
16 Riddiford Street, Newtown, tel 389-0470
A café by day, bistro by night, Malo is a Pacifica-themed cafe serving quality, homemade food – a well-above-average counter selection for starters. Brunch, lunch and dinner a la carte. Lively in the evenings. Nice relaxed vibe and a cross-section of clientele. Courtyard. Licensed. *Open Mon–Fri from 8am, Sat/Sun from 9am.*

EVA DIXON'S PLACE
Corner of Camperdown & Darlington Roads, Miramar, tel 388-8058
'Good old-fashioned nourishment to propel you through your modern day.' Not exactly on the beaten track, but well worth the detour for its dependable food and groovy retro décor. Excellent all day breakfast options, counter food and modern classics on the evening menu (Thurs–Sat only). Licensed. *Open Mon–Wed 7.30am–5pm, Thurs/Fri 7.30am–late, Sat 9am–late, Sun 9am–5pm.*

CHOCOLATE FISH
497 Karaka Bay Road, Scorching Bay, tel 388-2808
Set in a stunning location with a splendid view of the harbour entrance and Eastbourne, this is a perfectly evolved Kiwi tearoom. Yes, you can get fancy breakfast, panini and all that jazz, but you can also get a decent sausage roll, scones, milkshakes and ice cream. It's family-friendly and casual, and everyone likes it, including superstars (so rumour has it). Outside seating. *Open daily 9am–5pm.*

DINING OUT

Cheap Eats

Under $25 per person (two courses and coffee).

SATAY VILLAGE

58 Ghuznee Street, tel 801-8538

When our researchers were asked to name their favourite restaurants, Satay Village was mentioned more than any other. The consensus was 'consistent, fresh, tasty and fairly priced'. For those who like Malaysian cuisine or are keen to try it, we recommend laksa and roti all round. BYO. *Open Mon–Sat 11.30am–3pm & 5pm–10pm, Sun 5pm–10pm.*

MIYABI SUSHI

Willis Street Village, 142 Willis Street, tel 801-9688

Consistently delicious Japanese food, polite staff and great value keep Miyabi popular, despite its hiding place in Willis Street Village. A wide range of sushi, plenty of seafood and noodles all ways. Its terrific teriyaki comes with miso, salad and rice – a tasty, nutritious and inexpensive feast. Sake and Japanese beer also on offer. BYO/licensed. *Open Mon–Fri 11.30am–2.30pm & 5.30pm–late, Sat 5.30pm–late.*

SIEM REAP

101 Victoria Street, tel 472-3438

A delightful, centrally located Cambodian café with an intimate feel. Freshly prepared, delicious food, large portions, with plenty of vegetables in and around the menu. Good for a group outing, but you'll feel quite happy here on your own with a newspaper and a beer. BYO/licensed. Children welcome. *Open Mon–Sat 12pm–late.*

SAFFRON

132 Courtenay Place, tel 802-4990, www.saffronres.com

This is our version of the English curry house, and although there are several candidates in this category, it's the ambience and service that set Saffron apart (as well as a distinctly feminine touch!). An extensive menu features Tandoor specialities, set menus and several dishes announced 'first time in New Zealand'. Plenty of vegetarian options. BYO/licensed. *Open Mon–Sat 12pm–2.30pm & 5.30pm–late, Sun 5.30pm–10.30pm.*

STAMP AND GO

21 Majoribanks Street, Mt Victoria, tel 384-8244

Wellington's first and only Jamaican jerk shack has reggae grooves and a relaxed atmosphere. Specialities include jerk pork (marinated in pimento, chilli, brown sugar and rum), goat curry, tasty tortillas and cornbread baps. The best of the desserts is Boca Negra, 'black mouth' dark chocolate wedge with vanilla bean ice cream. Yum. Red Stripe beer, mango lassi and Cuban coffee also available. Licensed. *Open Tues–Sun 5pm–10pm.*

CATCH SUSHI BAR

48 Courtenay Place, tel 801-9352

Wellington's only sushi train. Yummy and good for you, in fact Jason says it's 'uplifting'! A la carte too, and takeways available. Japanese beers and tea. Licensed. *Open Mon–Sat lunch/dinner, Sun dinner.*

TANDOORI HERITAGE

23 Coutts Street, Kilbirnie, tel 387-7040

Authentic Indian Mughlai cuisine made using 600-year-old recipes, served in traditional 'thali' bowls. Inexpensive, with complimentary rice, potato, poppadom and pickle. Winner of numerous awards including Wellington's Best Indian Restaurant in 2002. Cosy interior and attentive service. Good vegetarian options. Children welcome. BYO/licensed. *Open Mon–Fri 11am–2.30pm & 4.30pm–9.30pm, Sat 4.30pm– 9.30pm, Sun 5.30pm–9.30pm.*

THE ORIGINAL THAI

155 The Parade, Island Bay, tel 383-5596

Authentic Thai cuisine, prepared by people who take pride in their work. The cosy interior is quiet and comfortable – perfect for families and groups. Although there are several Thai restaurants in and around the city, we rate this one tops. Deserved of its loyal clientele and well worth the short drive to the bay. BYO/licensed. *Open Tues–Sun 6pm–late.*

DINING OUT

For **bakeries**, most of which offer sit-down dining, see page 101.

Mid Range

Under $50 per person (two courses and coffee).

PRAVDA

107 Customhouse Quay, tel 473-8880

A slice of Eastern Europe in the capital, with high ceilings, chandeliers and mahogany furniture – this is one of the grandest dining rooms in town. Pravda offers breakfast, lunch and dinner a la carte – contemporary New Zealand flavours revised regularly to reflect the changing seasons. Many delicious things on offer: fresh fish, slow-roasted duck, lamb fillet, grilled tuna, hot smoked salmon, Caesar salad, plus plenty of vegetarian options and interesting desserts. Morning and afternoon tea also on offer. Licensed. *Open Mon–Fri 7.30am–late, Sat 9.30am–3pm.*

GREAT INDIA

141 Manners Street, tel 384-5755, www.greatindia.co.nz

Although there are many Indian restaurants in the city, the Great India is in a class of its own with its wonderful food, crisp white linen, faultless service and charming maitre-d'. Its authentic, fragrant cuisine from South Gujarat and Northern India is prepared by chefs trained in the UK – so what more can you say! The drinks list features many good wines, cocktails and 64 types of beer. Winner of far too many awards to list here. Children welcome. BYO/licensed. *Open Mon–Fri 12pm–2pm & 5pm–late, Sat/Sun 5pm–late.*

ANGKOR

43 Dixon Street, tel 384-9423, www.angkor.net.nz

The first Cambodian restaurant in Wellington, family-run Angkor has been a favourite since 1984. Cambodian cuisine is delicately spiced and aromatic, influenced both by its Asian neighbours and by the French. The diverse menu features plenty of vegetable accompaniments (and good vegetarian mains), making it somewhat lighter and more refined than much of Wellington's Asian cuisine. Its coconut-based house curry is delicate and delicious, and comes mild, medium or hot to your liking. A quiet and relaxed interior and attentive service. Licensed. *Open Mon–Fri 12pm–2.30pm & 5.30pm–late, Sat 5.30pm–late.*

CAPITOL

Corner of Kent Terrace & Majoribanks Street, tel 384-2855

Occupying a prime Kent Terrace corner, Capitol has made excellent use of its limited space, providing intimate dining with a fantastic panorama of Courtenay Place. It's a stylish restaurant with a simple menu delivering contemporary reworking of classic dishes, disctinctly Italian in style. Well selected, predominantly New Zealand wine can be enjoyed by the glass in most cases. Licensed. *Open Mon–Fri lunch from 12pm, Mon–Sat dinner from 6pm, Sat/Sun brunch 9.30am–2.30pm.*

REGAL CHINESE RESTAURANT

Level 1, 7–9 Courtenay Place, tel 384-6656

One of Wellington's many dim sum specialists, offering a lunch and evening menu of traditional Cantonese cuisine. The Regal's yum cha sessions are excellent, with the usual hustle and bustle reflecting thick and fast delivery of hot dishes, done well. Keep them coming and let the plates pile up! Excellent crispy duck. The Regal overlooks Courtenay Place, and has several comfortable and intimate dining areas. BYO/licensed. *Open daily 11am–2.30pm & 5.30pm–10.30pm.*

KOPI

103 Willis Street, tel 499-5570, www.kopi.co.nz

This upmarket Malaysian café stands out for its distinctly local approach to traditional cuisine, and considers itself 'upbeat', 'casual' and 'groovy'. If you haven't tried a roti in Wellington, then this is the place. Plain or rolled, stuffed or smothered, it's a meal in itself. A wide range of curries, noodle and rice dishes are prepared with attention to detail and subtlety of flavour. These are good reasons to go, but we also like Kopi for its Kapiti Feijoa ice cream, chocolate cake, fine cheeses, dessert wines, and a range of teas and excellent coffee. BYO/licensed. *Open daily 10am–late.*

CAFÉ ISTANBUL

156 Cuba Street, tel 385-4998, www.istanbul.co.nz

Family owned since opening in 1990, Istanbul has remained popular with locals for its extensive offering of Turkish cuisine, served in lively, ambient surroundings. Lots of big tables make it great for groups. A range of homemade breads and mezes are followed by meaty mains – lamb lovers will be happy here – with rice, bread, salad and garlic yoghurt featuring frequently. The veggie moussaka is tasty and should safely satisfy the herbivores. Various set menus also available. BYO/licensed. *Open Sun–Thurs 5.30pm–10pm, Fri/Sat 5.30pm–11pm.*

THE BEIJING

164 Riddiford Street, Newtown, tel 389-7988

If the food's good enough for the Chinese president (as it was on his November 2003 visit), it's good enough for us! This is a popular, family-run Newtown restaurant, serving northern Chinese cuisine, the hallmarks of which are a little more spice and a little more aroma. The 'Beijing roasted duck' is a speciality (order in advance), and vegetarians will be pleased with the extensive selection including 'mock duck'. Owners Liu Xin & Le Zhong Yin have asked this editor to pass on their sincere thanks to everyone who has supported them over the last seven years. BYO/licensed. *Open Tues–Sun 11.30am–2pm & 5.30pm–10pm.*

CHOW

45 Tory Street, tel 382-8585, www.chow.co.nz

A relative newcomer, quickly successful, Chow creates exciting Southeast Asian cuisine. What seems like a muddle of Cantonese, Japanese, Thai, Vietnamese and Malaysian flavours comes out as simple dishes done well. Order everything at once and share with your friends. A short but on-the-button dessert selection includes the delightfully aromatic baked chocolate mousse with cinnamon anglaise and vanilla bean ice cream – don't let this pud pass you by! We've heard several reports of inconsistent service, but the food will surely save the day. Licensed. *Open Mon–Fri lunch/dinner.*

Feed and feed back!

While we at *The Best of Wellington* are committed gluttons, we can't be everywhere at once. Please tell us where you dined and what made it stand out (sainthood or sickbag). Thank you, and bon appetit!

Top End

Over $50 per person, and worth every penny. Here are some of the best Wellington, and indeed New Zealand, has to offer. Bookings advisable.

LOGAN BROWN

Corner Cuba & Vivian Streets, tel 801-5114, www.loganbrown.co.nz
A grand 1920s banking chamber with lavishly ornate ceiling is home to Logan Brown, frequently touted as the best restaurant in town. This is friendly, accessible upmarket dining, and hosts Steve and Al sure know how to please. The food is generous, full flavoured and innovative with an extensive list of local and imported wines alongside. The bar (that doubles as an aquarium) has great drinks and tasting platters for those who just want to nibble. Lunch and pre-theatre bistro menu; live jazz on Sundays. Licensed/BYO Sunday. *Open Mon–Fri lunch from 12pm, daily for dinner from 6pm.*

CITRON

270 Willis Street, tel 801-6263
Absolutely first class, as you'd expect from renowned chef Rex Morgan. He and partner Wendy Hillyer, with their impeccable credentials and a stack of awards, opened Citron late in 2002. And how we love it. An intimate dining room, modern and minimalist, quiet, with low lighting, provides the perfect environment for enjoyment of a three-course set, or eight-course degustation menu. This is creative cuisine representing excellence in local flavour and freshness, beautifully prepared and presented with all the hallmarks of a first class restaurant – amuse bouche, petit fours, fine china, classy glassware and cutlery, quality linen, excellent wine knowledge and impeccable service. Memorable and highly recommended. Book well ahead. BYO/licensed. *Open Wed–Fri lunch from 12pm, Tues–Sat dinner from 6pm.*

MARIA PIA'S TRATTORIA

55 Mulgrave Street, tel 499-5590
Maria is a dynamo and an amazing advertisement for the Mediterranean diet and the slow-food movement. At her cosy trattoria, Maria makes authentic regional Italian food including

DINING OUT

fish soup, pasta and expertly cooked meat mains and game specials. Tiramisu, cheese and short coffee to round off. This is saucy, satisfying, mouthwateringly good food, prepared with passion. Organic ingredients are used wherever possible, and there's gluten-free, dairy-free and macrobiotic options for those who, like Maria, eat for health as well as indulgence. Italian wines. Licensed. *Open Tues–Fri lunch from 11.30am, Tues–Sat dinner from 5.30pm.*

ROXBURGH BISTRO

18 Marjoribanks Street, Mt Victoria, tel 385-7577,
www.roxburghbistro.co.nz

Set in a turn-of-the-century cottage, the Roxburgh is relaxed and unpretentious. Winner of numerous awards including the Michael Guy Eating Out Guide 'Best New Zealand Restaurant 2002'. The menu changes seasonally, and features modern and classic cuisine prepared with care and intelligence – Waikanae crab, mango and Thai coconut chicken salad, hare loin with pinot noir sauce, gingered rhubarb with mascarpone, meringue and feijoa sorbet and fine cheese. You'll want everything on the menu, and seafood lovers will delight. The wine list showcases many of New Zealand's best boutique wineries along with a splendid selection from abroad. Open fire in winter; private rooms available. Licensed. *Open Tues–Fri lunch/dinner, Sat dinner only.*

THE WHITE HOUSE

Upstairs, 232 Oriental Parade, tel 385-8555

Established in 1992, The White House has consistently been one of Wellington's top dining experiences. And it's situated in the middle of Oriental Bay with superb harbour views and a balcony. The menu has been described as 'modern, light, full of clean, clear flavours with a dash of Asian thrown in ... but with roots firmly anchored in the classic tradition.' Seafood is its speciality. While the food at The White House is undoubtedly the star, the front of house staff, extensive wine list and all round attention to detail make this a great treat for a special occasion. Licensed/BYO Sunday. *Open Mon–Tues dinner, Wed–Fri lunch/dinner, Sat/Sun dinner.*

Vegetarian

Warning: some of these serve non-vegetarian meals too!

ED'S JUICE BAR

95 Victoria Street, tel 478-1769

'I started Ed's after returning from Canada ... it was New Zealand's first juice bar and has grown steadily since its birth in 1998. Ed's is founded on good homely values. I really believe in keeping things local, fresh and providing good value for money. We just do what we feel is good and that seems to work for our customers ... Many great staff have all left a mark on the shop. It seems very much like it exists in its own micro-climate. A bit of a sanctuary, a juicy fun little place and somewhere I love and cherish as curator of my dreams slowly coming true.' Juices, smoothies, organic and vegan food. *Open Mon–Sun 8am–6pm, Sat/Sun 9am–5pm.*

GOPAL'S HARE KRISHNA

98 Victoria Street, tel 472-2233

Pure vegetarian Hare Krishna cuisine – predominantly Indian, wholesome, nutritious and inexpensive. There's a good-value all-day buffet, and a la carte specialities including samosa, pakora and thali (three curries with rice, chapati and chutney). Various salads, side dishes and desserts available, along with a wide range of freshly squeezed juices, smoothies, lassi and herbal teas. Take away some bhuja mix – yum. Children warmly welcomed. *Open Mon 11.30am–3pm, Tues–Fri 11.30am–3pm & 5pm–8pm, Sat 11.30am–3pm.*

SONAR TARI VEGETARIAN CAFÉ & JUICE BAR

179 Cuba Street, tel 384-2713

Healthy, wholesome and delicious. Vegetarian and vegan dishes from around the world served in peaceful surroundings by happy, helpful staff (resplendent in blue!). The likes of chilli, curry and stroganoff come in three bowl sizes, and plates boast burritos, nachos and the mushroom known as 'Portobello Mellow'. All-day brunch menu features buttermilk pancakes and free-range eggs, all ways. An ever-changing array of counter food available too, as are a wide range of juices, smoothies and lassis, coffee, chai and loose-leaf teas. *Open Mon/Tues/Thurs/Fri 8am–9pm, Wed/Sat 8am–3pm.*

DINING OUT

AUNTY MENA'S
167 Cuba Street, tel 382-8288
A mainstay of the Wellington veggie collective, Aunty Mena's is known for inexpensive, satisfying food in a relaxed café, half way down Cuba Street. The menu features mostly Asian cuisine including Thai, Malaysian and Chinese dishes. Plenty of tofu masquerading as meat. *Open Mon–Sat 11.30am–10pm, Sunday evenings.*

ARO CAFÉ
90 Aro Street, tel 384-4970
A spacious, relaxed café with a loyal following both in the neighbourhood and well beyond. Nice counter food, plus brunch, lunch and dinner a la carte. Interesting, wholesome food. Outside seating. Licensed. *Open Mon–Fri 7.30am–late, Sat/Sun 9am–late.*

REAL EARTH ORGANIC CAFÉ
98–110 Victoria Street, tel 470-7752
A contemporary, upbeat café serving tasty organic food, coffee, wine and beer. Good people-watching windows, and outside seating. Licensed. *Open Mon–Thurs 7.30am–4pm, Fri 7.30am–9pm, Sat/Sun 9am–3/4pm.*

NATURE VEGETARIAN FOOD
519 High Street, Lower Hutt, tel 560-4567
Really tasty home-cooked Asian vegetarian food, made with care and intelligence. Lovely spicy wontons, chewy mushroom 'meat' balls, fresh and delicious Thai broth, omelettes, noodles and rice dishes. Satisfying and excellent value for money. Nice people too. Phone orders and takeaways. *Open Tues–Wed 11am–8pm, Thurs–Sat 11am–9pm.*

Finding Felafel

On a felafel fact-finding mission, the best felafel in town was judged to be from **Phoenician Felafel** (Kent Terrace, near the Embassy Theatre) – an easy winner for its genuine, gently spiced mix and proper fillings (not drowning in dodgy chilli sauce). A clear runner up was **Cuba Kebab** (117 Cuba Street), who prepare, often smiling and consistently well, a dependable, fresh felafel served in clean, comfortable surroundings.

Feeding the Family

A selected handful across the spectrum.

ONE RED DOG
9 Blair Street, tel 384-9777
A lively gourmet pizza joint where noisy people fit in well, and a chance for you to have capers and anchovies while the kids have tomato and cheese. Main meals for children cost around $6.50 each. For dessert, children can fill up on yummy banana splits or ice cream and jelly. Drinks include fluffies, smoothies, juices and soft drinks. Colouring-in diversions and highchairs provided. Vegan dishes available on request. Licensed. *Open daily 10am–late.*

CLARKS CAFÉ
Wellington Central Library, 65 Victoria Street, tel 499-4444
If you're in town and need to fill a tummy or two, Clarks, in the central library, is reasonably priced and roomy. There's a good selection of tearoom-style food, an indoor play area and plenty of highchairs. Parents' room with comfortable seating; lift. *Open Mon–Fri 7.30am–7pm, Sat 9am–4.30pm, Sun 11am–4pm.*

WHITBY'S, AT THE JAMES COOK HOTEL GRAND CHANCELLOR
147 The Terrace (17th floor), tel 499-9500
Whitby's Sunday buffet is a popular family outing where children get to enjoy their own 'kids buffet'. Zappo the Magician entertains, and toys and colouring-in will keep everyone occupied. Children under 5 eat for free and, for those aged between 5–12, there's a $1.50 charge per year of age. Adults get their own buffet for $23. Free hotel car parking on Sunday. Licensed. *Open Sunday 11.30am–2.30pm.*

CAFÉ BASTILLE
16 Marjoribanks Street, tel 382-9559, www.dinehere.co.nz
For upmarket family dining, Café Bastille is a logical choice. They have a special children's menu ($9.90) so you get to sample some fine local cuisine, even with the kids in tow. Sistership of the brilliant Roxburgh Bistro next door, Bastille has a more informal atmosphere, and a menu of expertly prepared, reasonably priced French country classics. Fine wines. Licensed. *Open (children's menu) daily 5.30pm–7pm.*

DINING OUT

ELEMENTS
144 Onepu Road, Lyall Bay, tel 939-1292
A block from Lyall Bay beach, Elements warmly welcomes families
with its children's menu and safe tot's area. The outdoor seating and
ample parking make enjoying a beautiful Wellington day easy for
everyone. Relaxed atmosphere. Excellent cake cabinet. Daily specials
and lots of vegetarian options. BYO/licensed. *Open daily 9am–5.30pm.*

THE BACH
410 The Esplanade, Island Bay, tel 383-5120
Tucked between Red Rocks and Island Bay on Wellington's rugged
southern coast, The Bach makes a great excuse to drive around
the bays. The views are gorgeous and there's some good rock-pool
hopping along the shoreline. The Bach offers a well thought out
children's menu with a good range of choices. Prices range from $3–
$9. The grown-up menu is fairly standard, and there's a good cake
counter. Highchair available. Licensed. *Open Mon 9am–5pm, Tues–Sat
9am–10pm, Sun 9am–5pm.*

COBB & CO.
Cnr Tory Street & The Esplanade, Petone, tel 939-2622
The perfect place to take young children for a 'grown-up' outing. A
three course meal (for those under 12) costs $6.95 and tots under 3
eat for free. The menu offers cheeseburgers, chicken nibbles, pizza,
roast of the day and ice cream sundaes for dessert. Thick shakes
and 'cocktails' available including the ever-popular 'traffic light'.
Birthday parties a speciality. Highchairs provided. Licensed. *Open
daily 10am–3pm, 5pm onwards.*

PAVILION TEAROOMS AND RESTAURANT
Williams Park, Days Bay, Eastbourne, tel 562-7377
Lying in the middle of Williams Park, next to the Days Bay pier,
the Pavilion has long been part of the classic Wellington day trip.
There's heaps to do at the bay: feed the ducks, swim at the beach,
play sports on the lawn, walk in the bush, or just laze around.
The tearoom has ice cream, fish and chips and the like, while the
restaurant offers café-style dining. *Open daily.*

Sandwich Bars and Takeaways

PIZZA POMODORO

13 Leeds Street, off Dixon Street, tel 381-2929, www.pomodoro.co.nz

Authentic gourmet pizza, made by master Massimo Tolve. It comes square, crispy, fresh and fabulous from a wood-fired oven – our favourite. Choose from classics such as Marinara, Capricciosa and Quattro Formaggi, as well as calzone and saltimbocca available at lunchtime. Beer and wine also available. Deserving winner of 'Best Pizza' award in 2001 and 2002. Eat in or takeaway, and deliveries available in the city centre. *Open Mon 12pm–2pm, Tues–Fri 12pm–2pm & 5pm–10pm, Sat 12pm–2pm.*

HELL PIZZA

Tel 0800-TO-HELL, www.hell.co.nz

A hell of a lot better than your average pizza delivery. In fact great gourmet pizza, variations of which include Lust, Limbo, Greed, Sloth and Gluttony. They come in two sizes, with good vegetarian options, plus pasta, salads and desserts. Eat in or takeaway from any branch in the 'axis of evil' – Bond Street (city), Hataitai, Northland, Khandallah and Petone. They'll deliver for a few extra dollars. *Open daily from 5pm.*

SIR BREADWINS

144 Lambton Quay, tel 472-4803

This the best place to pick up a cheap lunch at the Lambton Quay end of town – perfect for that picnic on the Parliament lawn. At the back of the shop is the choose your own sandwich bar. The Vogel's version is particularly satisfying. Hot pies, scones and other homemade goodies available, as are milkshakes. Good value, nice people and popular as ever. *Open Mon–Fri 6am–4.30pm.*

MATSURI SUSHI

99 Victoria Street, tel 499-5782

A self-service sushi bar with ready-made takeaway packs. Matsuri is a popular lunch joint for its good value sushi, plus tempura and noodles too. *Tampopo*-esque hubbub and cheery service will satisfy the Japanoodlephiles. *Open Mon–Fri 9.30am–5.30pm, every second Sat 11am–3.30pm.*

DINING OUT

WELLINGTON TRAWLING SEAMARKET

220 Cuba Street, tel 384-8461

Pick-your-fillet fish and chips, straight from the fresh fish market. Dinner deals, family packs and burgers. *Open Mon–Thurs 7am–8pm, Fri 7am–9pm, Sat 7am–8pm, Sun 8am–8pm.*

SUPREMO TAKEOUTS

2a Moxham Avenue, Hataitai, tel 386–1037

Local winner 'Best Fish and Chip Shop' in 2002, Supremo cooks up crumbed fillets, kumara chips, gourmet, veggie and children's burgers, dinner packs and desserts. *Open Mon/Tues 11am–8.30pm, Wed/Thurs 10.30am–9pm, Fri/Sat 10.30am–9.30pm, Sun 11am–9pm.*

STARFISH

138 Molesworth Street, Thorndon, tel 499-9992

Quality fish and chips, a little out of the way, but well worth it. Lovely large fish fillets of various kinds. *Open Mon–Sat 11am–2pm & 4pm–9pm, Sun 4pm–9pm only.*

Good Pie!

Arguably the best *mince pie* in town is from the original and legendary **Patricia's** (298 The Parade, Island Bay). Patricia's little shop is a pastry-lover's paradise with its wall-to-wall warmers. Closer to town, **Crumbs** (corner Aitken & Mulgrave Streets) is also highly recommended for its quality pastry and good use of herbs, particularly sage. We liked their attention to detail.

The best *bacon and egg pie* (or is it a quiche?) will be found at the ever-popular **Arobake** (83 Aro Street) – quality bacon, a good cheesy flavour and a lovely wheel of tomato on top. **Patricia's** bacon and egg pie is the next best. It has a lid too, so it's officially a pie.

The quality *vegetarian pie* often proves elusive, but **Crumbs** shows true innovation here with its excellent kumara and feta pie, smattered with olives and sesame sprinkled. **Homestead Health** in Cuba Mall, however, must be commended for its commitment to the veggie pie trade. It stocks them hot and frozen, in several varieties, brought from Independent Bakeries in Christchurch. Wholesome, satisfying, and easy on the conscience.

(BASED ON A BLIND PIE TASTE-TEST, FIVE-PERSON PANEL, AUGUST 2003.)

Pubs, Bars and Live Music

How many great pubs and bars can this little city possibly have? Wellington is just the place where the ferry docks, right?

That may have been the case 15 years ago, but not any more. New Zealand's licensing laws were relaxed in the early 90s, bringing an end to 11pm closing. Wellingtonians liked this a lot, and quickly adapted to going out at midnight, rather than heading home. Courtenay Place came to life at about the same time. Yes indeed, this must-see marquee of city lights was once a backwater. The wind whistled through wall-to-wall warehouses, and the bus terminus was dark and creepy in the evening. Fortunately, a few far-sighted entrepreneurs saw potential; starting with warehouse apartments, they soon saw the opportunity to flog us grog as well. They quickly capitalised, and others soon flocked to join them. For a while it seemed like a new bar was opening every week, and even now it's hard to keep up.

The liquid lunch and late night scene has something for every taste and budget. Here we bring you our wrap-up, as well as listings for key bars and pubs most likely to please. There will always be new places to go, and locals will be glad to drag you along. But watch out, things change fast, and the bar you bonded with yesterday can be gone by tomorrow.

For music lovers, entertainment abounds, and gig listings can be found in the *Capital Times*, *The Package* (**www.thepackage.co.nz**), *The Dominion Post*, and individual websites as detailed.

PUBS, BARS, MUSIC

Lounges and Cocktail Bars

The Wellington bar scene has come along in leaps and bounds in the last decade or so. There's a flotilla of fabulous lounge bars, each with an interesting décor and special draw, but all sharing the common elements that ensure they flourish: low-light, nice tunes and fine drinks. While all are obliged to offer you something to snack on, many go the extra mile and make a meal of it.

The **Matterhorn** can be credited with leading the charge of Cuba Street lounge bars, being unapologetically young and hip, and setting the standard for many that have followed. Just up the mall is **Good Luck**, the ultimate 'in the know' bar, and one of the best for a close dance or kissing in a corner.

Courtenay Place will see you spoilt for choice, especially if you love the sound of the cocktail shaker. **Motel**, once the most insufferably cool bar in town, seems to have now outgrown the dubious cachet of turning away Liv Tyler and settled down to making good drinks. **Mercury Lounge**, which starts out slow and picks up later on, is notable for quality DJs. Lucky old **Jet** enjoys a splendid corner location, and while it might seem just that little bit too trendy, its service is tops and clientele quite diverse.

MATTERHORN

106 Cuba Street, tel 384-3359, www.matterhorn.co.nz
A Cuba Street institution, the Matterhorn recently reopened after the longest makeover in history. We say it was worth the wait. While the famous courtyard is now almost totally closed in and the capacity has increased, the bar and bistro still have a cosy feel. Live music remains key to the Matterhorn experience, with bands on Wed/Sun (mainly funk–soul–jazz), and DJs Thurs–Sat. The kitchen is open from brunch till late; the food is good and genuinely innovative. Exemplary wine list. Open fire in winter.
Open Mon–Fri 9am–late, Sat/Sun 10am–late.

GOOD LUCK

Basement, 126 Cuba Street, tel 801-9950
Wellington's Chinese opium den, without the opium, and not in China. Good Luck's interior has won praise from all over the country

– we think it's verrrrry sultry! Good Luck specialises in cocktails, but have a great range of other drinks too. Full Thai menu, presented in co-operation with the neighbouring restaurant, so it's better than average bar food. Table service in the lounge section, with dancing on the cosy dance floor – DJs kick off after 10pm. There's no signage for Good Luck, so ask a Cubaphile where to find it. *Open daily 4.30pm– late.*

MOTEL
Forresters Lane (off Tory Street), tel 384-9084
Tres chic. Quality cocktails and ambient décor. Handsome people, and sometimes hard to get in. Staff are on the ball, and we like the bassy beats. Yes, it is down that dark alley. *Chow* next door has good modern Asian food (see DINING OUT). *Open Wed–Sat 7pm–3am.*

MERCURY LOUNGE
46 Courtenay Place, tel 384-6737
A haven away from the hustle and bustle, Mercury is a dark and intimate lounge bar where you can talk without having to shout. There are DJs Thurs–Sat, including some of Wellington's favourites. *Open Mon–Fri 5pm–late, Sat 6pm–3am, Sun 7pm–late.*

JET BAR AND LOUNGE
Corner Allen Street & Courtenay Place, tel 803-3324
Home of the jetset, and a stellar bar in every sense. They've got a very stylish interior, separate lounges and private booths, plus a well-presented selection of quality drinks including really juicy fruit cocktails – with or without the alcohol. Professional service. All day bar snacks. Outside seating. *Open daily 3pm–6am.*

LIE LOW
286 Willis Street
It's lying low because it's in the path of the proposed motorway, and will probably be bowled soon in the name of progress (*Bodega* has already moved out … see next page). In the meantime though, Lie Low is a lovely late night cocktail lounge, with kitsch décor and great music. Brunch at the weekends. And your hosts know how to look after folk too. *Open Thurs 8pm–late, Fri 8pm–late, Sat 9am–4pm/8pm–late, Sun 9am–4pm.*

PUBS, BARS, MUSIC

Live Music

Wellington has a thriving music scene. While it has always been active, recent industry initiatives and growing support by the public has seen a boom in Kiwi music, video production and artists on tour. It's exciting and we're loving every minute of it – and so can you!

The **Cuba Street** area has numerous music venues hosting a range of Kiwi and international acts. **Indigo** is a popular choice for touring bands, being a mainstay of the Wellington scene in various guises for more than 40 years. It normally springs to life around 11pm, but the recent addition of a sun-drenched balcony should see it become a daytime haunt as well. Nearby **Valve** is also a late night starter and a good place to spot up-and-coming talent. It's a small rock venue with a big history (check out the drumsticks over the bar), and can certainly throw up the odd surprise. Around the corner in Ghuznee Street is arguably Wellington's most famous bar, **Bodega** (see opposite). Many who start out in Cuba Street will end up in nearby Edward Street at **Studionine** or **Subnine** – two venues hosting local and foreign stars of the dance music scene. Kid Loco, Carl Cox, Ashley Beedle and Mr Scruff, to name a few, have all played here. **Pound** is also a popular late-nighter, welcoming all but catering specifically for the gay-lesbian-alterative scene.

Bridging the **Cuba–Courtenay** gap is **Diva** on Dixon Street, which has trodden a fine line for years – a restaurant early in the evening, it transforms into a popular dance spot later in the evening. Diagonally across the way is **Molly Malones**, Wellington's Irish music home and a safe bet for live acts every night of the week.

Music is pretty much guaranteed in the **Courtenay Place** bars, but a few do it better and more often than others. **Amba** remains the most likely to have live music on any given night, with regular bookings for jazz, swing, soul and funk. Newcomer **Sandwiches** has quickly found favour for its commitment to the dance music scene and a brilliant sound system – easily the best in town.

For more about Kiwi music, try ... Live (Wellington's music mag) or
www.wellingtonlive.co.nz www.bands.co.nz www.spacific.net
www.noizyland.co.nz www.nzmusic.org.nz www.midi.org.nz

Beats and Bubbles at Bodega

Originally located in a demolition-threatened building at the top of Willis Street, over a glorious decade Bodega became the capital's premier live music venue. Despite only being able to hold around 150 people, (people who didn't mind being crammed in like sardines with loads of secondhand smoke), almost all of New Zealand's top bands and a few foreign stars played 'The Bodge' at some stage. Eventually it was time to leave and find somewhere less likely to have a bulldozer drive through the back wall. The new-look Bodega — three times the size and 33 times less lived in than its predecessor — was greeted with some trepidation, but the bar's loyal locals have followed it down the road. So have the bands, now revelling in a much better space with more room and superior equipment. Bodega remains the city's best mid-range live music venue, and its enthusiastic support of micro-breweries, including local Tuatara, makes it a bar equally beloved of beer drinkers.

Bodega, 101 Ghuznee Street, tel 384-8212, open daily 4pm–late.

Dominion Post

Bodega's bar is moved with music as it makes the short journey to its new home, in September 2002. A band of locals turned out to prop it up, which made for a nice change. Owner Fraser McInness was heard to express concern about the effects of 'ultraviolet radiation' on the beautiful worn timber, and one staffer remarked that although it was probably a 'shock' for the bar, at least it had a day to prepare after punters drank it dry the night before. Bodega's move was prompted by the impending inner-city bypass which will see a six-lane intersection in its place (see page 163).

INDIGO
171 Cuba Street, tel 801-6797, www.indigobar.co.nz
A mainstay of the local music scene with live entertainment Tues–
Sat. The Wellington Comedy Club holds regular Thursday sessions,
with Friday and Saturday nights dedicated to local, national and
international music acts. Cover charge may apply at these times.
Cosy ambience; balcony; pool table. *Open Mon–Sat 3pm–late.*

VALVE
154 Vivian Street, tel 385-1630
Home of a wide range of live music – rock, punk, metal, reggae,
drum 'n' bass, hip-hop and trance. A musician-friendly venue with
4000 watt PA, studio monitoring and effects. Intelligent lighting.
'True underground spirit.' *Open late.*

STUDIONINE
Level 1, 9 Edward Street, tel 384-9976, www.studionine.co.nz
Underground dance music venue presenting regular local, New
Zealand and international artists – see their website for listings.
Open Sat/Sun 11pm–late.

POUND
Level 1, Oaks Complex, Dixon Street, tel 384-6024, www.pound.co.nz
Mal and Scotty own and operate Pound, Wellington's only gay-
lesbian-alternative nightclub. A popular watering hole with diverse
clientele, Pound is known for its friendly atmosphere and great
personalities. There's a big dance floor and a crew of DJs. Regular
show nights are Friday at midnight, and Saturday at 2am. Pool
tables, dartboard and pinball. *Open Tues–Fri 4.30pm–late, Sat 8pm–late, Sun
5pm–late.*

MOLLY MALONES
Corner Courtenay Place & Taranaki Street, tel 384-2896
Molly Malones is Wellington's original Irish pub with live music
every night. Downstairs offers the pick of Wellington's Celtic bands
and a lively session on Monday nights. The Dubliner bar upstairs
has music in the weekends and 110 whiskies. A good place for foot-
stomping fun or hair-raising jigs and reels. Guinness and Kilkenny
on tap; bar and restaurant dining. Big screen. *Open daily 11am–late.*

SANDWICHES

8 Kent Terrace, tel 385-7698, www.sandwiches.co.nz

A welcome and long-awaited addition to the Wellington dance music scene, Sandwiches is a lounge and club of multi-flavoured entertainment. The cream of local and national bands and DJs can be heard on New Zealand's best sound system, with big-name international performers joining in on occasion. A unique interior and superior design helps make Sandwiches a friendly and fun place to enjoy warm hospitality and dance music. Door sales always available. *Open Tues–Sat 3pm–late.*

AMBA

21 Blair Street, tel 801-5212, www.amba.co.nz

Jewel in the Wellington jazz crown? Proabably so. Amba's commitment to live jazz, as well as funk, reggae and dub keeps it popular. It's a nice space, unpretentious and a good choice for meeting your mates for a beer and a boogie. Live bands daily Wed–Sun. Full menu; lots of imported beer and 'carefully selected' wines. *Open daily 3pm–6am.*

Lambton Quay

Lambton Quay is the business end of town where long lunches stretch well into the afternoon and the city's suits and civil servants can be found after a hard day at the office. There are more than 20 pubs and bars at this end of town, several with live music later in the week, and many with excellent food.

Wellington's **waterfront** is an obvious destination for those seeking a watering hole, but as you'll see, bars and cafés have been slow to migrate towards the harbour; six lanes of Jervois Quay traffic is often blamed. However, **Shed 5** and **Dockside** are well worth the effort, both sitting pretty upmarket on the water's edge, and both known for good food. **Chicago** is lively, more laid-back and big on sport.

There are plenty of pubs on the parallel drags **Lambton Quay** and **Featherston Street**. Close to the Beehive and the first on the Quay is the **Occidental**, a pleasant pub with good grub and live music on Thursday and Friday. Further up on Featherston Street are several options within a stone's throw of each other, the highlight of which is **Leuven**, a Belgian-themed bar, bustling at night and with sidewalk seating, popular on sunny days. The Irish-themed **Black Harp**, with its homely interior, traditional fare and live music is the place to go to meet real live Kiwi regulars enjoying their local.

The best of The Terrace is **Liquidate**, a trendy little lunchtime joint that comes alive in the evenings, with DJs on Friday nights. Around the corner on Willis Street is **The Malthouse**, beer-lover's paradise and the best balcony in town.

SHED 5
Queens Wharf, tel 499-9069, www.shed5.co.nz
Great seafood on the waterfront. Built in 1888 as a woolshed, Shed 5 is one of Wellington's oldest remaining wharf stores. This beautifully restored building boasts a spacious interior and covered courtyard. There's a large selection of fine beverages at the bar, or in the restaurant: recommended. *Open daily 11am–3pm, 6pm–late.*

LEUVEN BELGIAN BEER CAFÉ
135 Featherston Street, tel 499-2939
Our Belgian connection brings us mussels and chips with lashings of beer including Duvel, Hoegaarden, Leffe, Belle-Vue and Stella Artois. Housed in a century-old building, the authentic 'brown' interior boasts an interesting array of artefacts to set the scene. It's centrally located and easy to find, making it a good meeting place – perfect for that long Lambton-end lunch. An evening set menu offers several choices for three Belgian-style courses, and the breakfast menu has waffles, crêpes and omelettes. Outside seating available. *Open Mon–Fri 7am–late, Sat/Sun 10am–late.*

THE MALTHOUSE
47 Willis Street, tel 499-4355, www.themalthouse.co.nz
One of the first pubs to embrace the now thriving boutique beer market, The Malthouse proudly serves 26 beers on tap (at last count) including local brew, Tuatara, and lots of other Kiwi specials. The $5 tasting tray gives you a chance to sample five at once. Its balcony is pleasant for an alfresco lunch and affords excellent people-watching. *Open Mon–Sat lunch–late.*

Watching the Big Game

We love to watch sport and, odds on, the big game will fill up the pubs. Here's your best bet for watching the game without squinting or craning your neck. You might even get a seat.

Close together on Cuba Street, **JJ Murphy's** and **Hotel Bristol** can be relied on to screen the big game, particularly if it's rugby. They have two big screens apiece, plenty of room, and are perfect for pool and a pint. Both also do pub grub and host live music. The new-look **Lovelocks** is home to the city's serious sports fantatics.

The English-themed **Courtenay Arms** looks after footy fans of all kinds. It'll often be packed with passionate ex-pats swilling British ale. Around the corner, The **Sports Café** offers a more testosterone-fuelled environment for watching the game (and is allegedly good for a steak). **The Grand**, a bit of a barn, is the place for partisans who like it lively.

JJ MURPHY & CO.

119 Cuba Street, tel 384-9090

Irish-themed pub with Murphy's Irish Red and Stout on tap, plus an Irish menu available around meal times. Two large floors, seven pool tables and two big screens. Live music Wed–Sat (except big-game nights). *Open daily 10am–late.*

LOVELOCKS SPORTS BAR

12 Bond Street, tel 473-1311

Wellington's original sports bar: 'if you like sport, you'll love it' says the manager. Lovelocks has recently been refurbished and is now a welcoming place for strangers to meet some of Wellington's keenest punters and best-informed sports fans. There's a big screen, TAB (betting agency), poker machines, two pool tables, a dart board and bar food. *Open Mon–Sat 11am–late, Sun 1pm–8pm.*

COURTENAY ARMS ALE HOUSE

26–32 Allen Street, tel 385-6908

An English-style pub with decor to match. Wellington's most expansive range of imported ales on tap such as Boddington's, Old Speckled Hen, Young's Ramrod and Chocolate Stout, Tetley's English Ale and Newcastle Brown, and John Smith's. British pub-style food

PUBS, BARS, MUSIC

too (Shepherd's Pie, Bangers & Mash ... you get the drift). Pool tables, dart boards, juke box, open fire, big sports screen and gaming lounge. Proudly focused on football. Dance floor. *Open Mon–Sat 12pm– late, Sun 12.30pm–late.*

THE REALM TAVERN

7 Moxham Avenue, Hataitai, tel 386-3607, www.therealm.co.nz
Situated in the middle of Hataitai village, The Realm is a popular place for watching the big game and is 'better known as the home of Wellington rugby'. Good menu. Highly recommended by many locals. Daily two-for-one meals and happy hours, plus $5 brunch every weekend. *Open Mon–Fri 3pm–late, Sat/Sun 10am–late.*

A Few Other Favourites

IMBIBE ANTIPASTO

6 Swan Lane, (between Cuba & Marion Streets), tel 385-7060, www.imbibe.net.nz
'Knowledgeable friendly staff, good wine list, yummy food, vegetarian choices and delicious dessert,' says one punter. Imbibe is a wine bar serving a well-selected, predominantly Kiwi wine list, most available by the glass. Its sexy red and black interior and cool tunes create an ambience perfect for the enjoyment of their victuals. Excellent effort in the food department: innovative antipasto platters as well as a cheese board and chocolate fondue. Some courtyard seating. *Open Mon–Sat 4.30pm–late.*

BRAVA

2 Courtenay Place, tel 384-1159
Underneath Downstage Theatre, Brava is a bar and restaurant with generally good fare and a raft of regular patrons. It can get a bit packed pre- and post-show, but either side of the main bill it tends to thin out and become a place where you can enjoy a glass of red and wait for Godot. The lighting's nice, and frequently changing artwork and professional service make it welcoming to a wide range of people. Cocktails; brunch until 5pm on weekends. *Open Mon–Fri 4pm–late, Sat/Sun 9am–late.*

BALL ROOM

68 Courtenay Place, tel 801-7994

A pool hall and popular melting pot, the Ball Room has 34 pool tables available, either $10 per hour or $2 per game. Here you'll find a cross-section of people, most there for the love of the game. All sorts of music played quite loudly. *Open daily 11.30am–late.*

THE POSTIE'S WHISTLE

Corner Ganges Road & Agra Crescent, Khandallah, tel 479-4157

It's our Rover's Return, only it's carpeted and the beer is real. Choose from Tetley's, Boddingtons, John Smith's, Kilkenny and Murphy's on tap, as well as Kiwi beers. Relaxed and unpretentious, warm and comfortable, the perfect place to take mum and dad. Reasonably priced traditional pub fare. *Open daily 11am–11pm, 11am–midnight Sat/Sun.*

SPEIGHTS ALE HOUSE

285 Tinakori Road, Thorndon, tel 472-1320, www.shepherds.co.nz

A well-presented modern Kiwi pub in New Zealand's oldest hotel, *The Shepherd's Arms* (a beautifully restored colonial clasic). 'Southern man' interior and a couple of largish TV screens. Crowd-pleasing pub grub: carefully prepared, good value meals. *Open daily from 11am.*

Shepherd's Arms Hotel

PUBS, BARS, MUSIC

Positively Wellington Tourism (Nick Servian)

Well-being and Body Beautiful

A bit what you fancy does you good, of course, but you've got to give a little back to that body of yours. Here we bring you some ways to relax, revitalise and luxuriate.

Wholefoods and Organics

COMMONSENSE ORGANICS
260 Wakefield Street, tel 384-3314, www.commonsenseorganics.co.nz
Wellington's largest selection of organic foods including fresh produce. Commonsense caters to folk with food allergies, and sells environmentally sound products for health care, household and garden. All GE-free of course, with minimal and recycled packaging. Owners Marion and Jim started out in organics in 1975, opening the shop in 1991, '... our dream of changing the world remains.' *Open Mon–Fri 9am–7pm, Sat 9am–6pm, Sun 10am–6pm.*

HOMESTEAD HEALTH FOODS
112 Cuba Mall, tel 802-4425, www.homesteadhealth.co.nz
Right in the middle of Cuba Street is a favourite natural health products store (established 1973) stocking nutritional supplements, aromatherapy, homeopathics, natural cosmetics, wholefoods (both organic and non-organic) and environmentally friendly household cleaning products. Knowledgeable staff can provide advice and direct you to best products for you. Special foods for those with allergies (wheat, gluten, dairy, egg and sugar free), and other dietary requirements catered for. *Open Mon–Thurs 8.30am–6pm, Fri 8.30am–7pm, Sat 10am–4pm, Sun 10am–3pm.*

Natural Therapies

SIMILLIMUM HOMEOPATHIC PHARMACY

20 Panama Street, tel 499-9242, www.arnica.co.nz

Simillimum (meaning the most perfect remedy) was started in 1995 to provide a range of high quality, traditionally prepared remedies. The pharmacy is run and owned by pharmacists Shirley Gay and Michael Dong, who are also classically trained homeopaths. 'The pharmacy provides a place where people can come and experience the magic of homeopathy. We stock a wide range of books on homeopathy and our open dispensary means you can watch your remedies being made. We welcome visitors and are always keen to answer your questions about homeopathy!' *Open Mon–Fri 9am–5.30pm, Sat 10am–3pm.*

BOTANICALS HERBAL DISPENSARY

3 Moxham Avenue, Hataitai, tel 386-2223, email botanicals@actrix.co.nz

Free dispensary advice on herbal medicine and natural healthcare, and stockists of an extensive range of medicinal herbs, organic herbal teas, handmade creams, essential oils, Bach remedies and chemical-free body and hair products. Also offer massage and therapies including aromatherapy and reiki. Herbal medicine and naturopathic consultations; individual herbal mixtures made. *Open Tues–Fri 10am–5.30pm, Sat 10am–1pm.*

NATURAL HEALTH CENTRE

Level 2, 53 Courtenay Place, tel 385-4342, www.nhc.co.nz

The Natural Health Centre has more than 20 practitioners offering services in a safe and comfortable environment including health consultancy, counselling, homeopathy, psychotherapy, osteopathy, cranial-sacral therapy, Chinese orthopedics, corporal therapy, acupuncture, physiotherapy, reiki, reflexology, Bowen technique, shiatsu and one-to-one yoga. Experienced massage therapists with specialisation in deep tissue, sports massage, relaxation and remedial massage for muscle conditions. *Open Mon–Sat, appointments required.*

MANUKA HEALTH CENTRE

11 Hector Street, Petone, tel 939-1299

The Manuka Health Centre was established in April 2001 in response to a growing consumer demand for complementary healthcare combined with conventional medical family practice. The owner, Dr Mark Austin, graduated from Otago University, Dunedin, in 1983 and he describes his practice as integrated medicine: combining the best aspects of both conventional and complementary therapies. Joining him at the centre is Dr Susanna Kent, another integrative GP, as well as practitioners offering counselling, osteopathy, chiropractic, homeopathy, traditional Chinese medicine, Neurolinguistic Programming, hypnotherapy, Bach flowers, reiki, Bowen therapy and HUGS Diet/lifestyle advice. *Open Mon–Fri, by appointment.*

EAST DAY SPA

Level 2, Tramways Building, 1 Thorndon Quay, tel 473-3611, www.eastspa.com

Focusing on natural, holistic and organic beauty treatments, East offers a combination of Eastern-influenced massage with other traditional exotic therapies including facials, exfoliations, wraps, heat treatments, hydrotherapy and beauty therapy. 'Sometimes all you want is a little bit of peace and quiet ... a buffer between timelessness and the stressful urgencies of everyday life'. *Open daily, appointments required.*

BODY BALANCE

302 Tinakori Road, Thorndon, tel 499-7255

Massage therapy in a relaxed, homely environment in Thorndon, delivered by highly qualified practioners – Robyn, Petra and Luise. Modalities offered include shiatsu, Bowen technique, Jin Shin Jyutsu, reiki, aromatherapy, reflexology and acupressure. *Open Mon–Sat, appointments required.*

The *Therapeutic Massage Association*, www.tmanz.org.nz is an industry group that looks after massage professionals in New Zealand. Its website lists all members, as well as offers information on all the different massage types ('modalities').

Yoga and Meditation

YOGA IN DAILY LIFE

Level 1, 21 Jessie Street, tel 801-7012, www.yogaindailylife.org.nz
Yoga in Daily Life is a holistic system aimed at fostering the physical, mental, social and spiritual health and well-being of all, and suitable for people of all ages and levels of fitness, including the ill and convalescent. Six-week progressive courses: beginners, intermediate and yoga for pregnancy. Casual yoga and meditation classes; rural retreats. Cost $5.50–$13 per class. Open Mon–Sat. See website for timetable, telephone or call in.

WELLINGTON BUDDHIST CENTRE

64 Cambridge Terrace, tel 384-1334, www.fwbo.org.nz
Introductory Buddhism and meditation courses, drop-in classes, festivals, country retreats, and other activities. Call for details and timetable, or visit the website.

BODH GAYA BUDDHIST CENTRE

Level 1, 88 Manners Mall, tel 473-3221, www.meditate.org.nz
'A facility where people can learn about meditation and the Buddhist way of life,' the Bodh Gaya centre offers a range of drop-in classes, day courses and special events suitable for beginners and experienced meditators alike. Casual visitors welcome. Telephone or visit the website for timetables or more information.

TE ARO ASTANGA YOGA

110 Cuba Street, tel 388-8024
Scheduled classes for beginners onwards, and six-week beginners course. Telephone for details and timetable. Cost for casual classes $12. Open Mon–Fri and Sun.

YOGA CENTRAL

120 Cuba Street, tel 385-1461
Iyengar style yoga, daily classes from beginners to advanced, casual classes and five-week beginners class. Telephone for details and timetable. Cost for casual classes $15. Open daily.

WELLINGTON HATHA YOGA CENTRE
134 Cuba Street, tel 385-6000
Casual classes, six-week courses at four levels, yoga for pregnancy
and private tuition. Telephone for details and timetable. *Cost for
casual classes $12. Open* daily.

SRI CHIMNOY MEDITATION CLASSES
Tel 384-2713
Six-class introductory meditation courses held at 44 Cable Street
(opposite Te Papa). *Cost* free.

ZHINENG QIGONG
Tel 499-1216, www.qigongtrust.org.nz
(Pronounced 'chee-gong'.) Moving meditation for clearing blockages
allowing the 'qi' to flow, for better health and self-realisation.
Classes by Master Liu, held at the Buddhist Centre on Cambridge
Terrace and Thorndon Tennis Club. Individual healing by
appointment. All classes open to beginners. Telephone or visit their
website for details.

Beautiful Bodies

LAVAGE
174 Cuba Street, tel 801–6881, www.lavageint.co.nz
Pure and natural body care, all made in New Zealand including some
own-brand – wonderful natural handmade soaps, delightful lotions
and more. Inexpensive and luxurious options available. This shop
smells divine, and so can you. *Open Mon–Thurs 10am–6pm, Fri 10am–7pm,
Sat 10am–5pm, Sun 11am–4pm.*

LIVING NATURE
195 Lambton Quay, tel 499-5060, www.livingnature.com
Natural skincare and cosmetics made by one of the world's only
makers of paraben- and synthetic-free products. All are made in
Kerikeri using a number of key New Zealand native ingredients
such as manuka and flax gel. They are GE-free, not tested on animals
and contain no animal-derived ingredients other than beeswax and
honey. It's fragrant and it feels good. Recyclable, environmentally
friendly packaging. *Open Mon–Fri 10am–6pm, Sat/Sun 10am–4pm.*

PURE BEAUTY

236 Oriental Parade, tel 384-7378, www.pureonline.co.nz
(Also at 1/310 Tinakori Road.) Two high quality salons offering
a wide range of beauty therapies including facials, body wraps,
tanning, and eye, hand and foot treatments. Hair tinting,
bleaching and removal, and makeovers also available. Delightful
half-day packages would make a splendid gift. Stockist of
Thalgo, Vitaman (especially for men), Trucco, St Tropez and the
highly sought after locally made Hema skincare range. *Open daily,
appointments required.*

URBAN SANCTUARY

3 Plimmer Steps, tel 471-1144, www.facial.co.nz
Award-winning Decleor beauty clinic and day spa for an experience
of pampering and relaxation to rejuvenate the body, mind and
spirit. Facials, aromatherapy, massage, body wraps, airbrush
spray tanning, half-day and full-day packages and beautifully gift-
wrapped vouchers. *Open Mon–Sat, appointments required.*

BUOY

Skye Garden, Majestic Tower, 100 Willis St, tel 472-3430, www.buoy.co.nz
The best haircuts in town in the most beautiful salon. Luxurious
and priced accordingly. *Open daily, appointments essential.*

JUST TEASING

287 Cuba Street, tel 801-7775
Creative hairdressing in a relaxed atmosphere, suitable for the
whole family and those who want to get funky. Go and see Gale
hanging in there at the historic upper end of Cuba Street. *Open daily,
appointments not always necessary.*

BARBERS ...

A handful recommended in the city centre; no appointment
necessary; cost around around $25.

Swan Barbers, 69 The Terrace, tel 499-9090
Norris Barbers, 31 Waring Taylor Street, tel 499-9080
Mike Fleming Village Barber, 5/142 Willis Street, tel 801-5945
Clubman Hairstylists, Left Bank, 305 Cuba Mall, tel 384-7232

Tattoo and Body Piercing

FLESH WOUND
253 Cuba Street, tel 801-6532, www.fleshwound.co.nz
Wellington's only specialist studio offering piercing, jewellery,
branding and scarification. More than 18 years' experience.
Exceptional hygiene standards and aftercare support. The widest
range of piercing-related jewellery and accessories. 'Word of mouth
brings in customers from around the world. Safe, accurate, clean,
friendly and informative.' *Open Tues–Sat, appointments required.*

TATTOO CITY
1st Floor, 124 Cuba Mall, tel 801-5403
'Our studio has a diverse range of artist with local knowledge of
Maori tattoo (ta moko) through to international experience through
regular travel to conventions, giving us a chance to source any latest
advances in styles, technique and hygiene practice, but most of all
we get to experience first hand the different cultures and flavours
that link the modern and ancient tattoo worlds ... through this we
have made friends with some of the best tattoo artists the world has
to offer, who visit us to share their art with our clients and friends.
But most of all, we love what we do.' *Open Mon–Sat, appointments required.*

ROGER'S TATTOOART
198 Cuba Street, tel 384-5242
Roger's studio is the mainstay of Wellington tattoo, having been
in its Cuba Street location since 1977. Roger is an internationally
recognised tattoo artist, versatile and happy to take on big custom
work. Tom shares his studio. Come in, browse and chat about your
masterpiece at any time. *Open Mon–Sat from noon, appointments required.*

UNDERGROUND ARTS
29 Wigan Street, tel 385-2185
Two tattoo artists including Wellington's only lady tattooist. Retail
outlet offers a wide range of unusual adornments by New Zealand
artists including jewellery, T-shirts, ornaments, paintings and
posters. *Open Tues–Sat 12pm–5.30pm.*

For **National Tattoo Museum**, see page 19.

Positively Wellington Tourism (Nick Servian)

Travel and Transport

As New Zealand's central transport hub for air, rail, coach and the northern Cook Strait ferry terminal, all roads lead to Wellington! Once you're here, you'll find it easy to explore our compact city, whether on foot or by one of many other means outlined in the following pages.

The *Wellington Visitor Information Centre* has timetables and lots of other transport information, and offers no-fee bookings for many services. Bookings can also be made at the railway station ticket office, or direct from the service operator.

Scenic tours can be found in ATTRACTIONS AND ACTIVITIES.

Ridewell tel 801-7000
freephone 0800-801-700

Getting to and from Wellington

Air

Experience the excitement of Wellington air!

Wellington is no more than an hour's flight from anywhere in New Zealand, and the airport is a mere 15-minute drive from the city centre.

Wellington International Airport is New Zealand's aviation hub, handling more than 3.5 million passengers a year. The light and airy terminal building offers good shopping, reasonable food, currency exchange and other facilities. Long-term parking is available from $12 per day. See **www.wlg-airport.co.nz** for more information.

AIR NEW ZEALAND

TravelCentre, corner Grey Street & Lambton Quay, tel 474-8950, freephone 0800-737-000, www.airnewzealand.co.nz
New Zealand's airline has services to all major and many smaller domestic destinations, as well as trans-Tasman and around the globe. Book in advance or online for good discounts. A one-way advance ticket across Cook Strait is around $65.

SOUNDS AIR

Tel 0800-505-005, www.soundsair.com
Inexpensive frequent flights across Cook Strait. A scenic treat for $79 one-way ($55 specials). Charter service available. Locally owned and operated for 17 years.

ORIGIN PACIFIC AIRWAYS

Tel 0800-302-302, www.originpacific.co.nz
Based in Nelson, locally owned Origin Pacific offers scheduled services to major domestic destinations. Competitive fares, with good discounts – pay as little as $50 one way across the strait.

QANTAS AIRWAYS

2 Hunter Street, tel 0800-808-767, www.qantas.co.nz
Flies from Wellington direct to Auckland, Hamilton, Nelson and Christchurch, and indirect to Rotorua, Dunedin, Queenstown and Invercargill. Also services trans-Tasman and international routes.

There are several options for getting from the *airport to the city*.

- **Taxi** – around $20 to the city centre.

- **Bus** – the *Stagecoach Flyer* runs between the airport and Upper Hutt, stopping at all major stops en route, and every city stop from Courtenay Place to Thorndon. An adult fare to the city centre is $4.50. For more information on the Flyer, see GETTING AROUND THE CITY.

- **Shuttle** – several companies offer door-to-door services for around $10–12 per person to the city, and $25 to Lower Hutt (additional passengers to the same location $2–$5).

Rail

TRANZ SCENIC
Tel 0800-872-467, www.tranzscenic.co.nz
New Zealand's national railway network, doing the best they can, and well.

- **Auckland–Wellington:** the *Northerner* is a daily overnight service between Auckland and Wellington (departs Auckland 8.40pm, Wellington 7.50pm). It will save you the cost of a night's accommodation, and although there are no sleeping carriages the reclining seats are reasonably comfortable. The *Overlander* is the daytime equivalent, departing Auckland 8.30am, and Wellington 8.45am. Substantial discounts for advance bookings, subject to availability, eg $64 Northerner, $73 Overlander one-way. Be sure to ask for the latest deal.

- **Palmerston North–Wellington:** the *Capital Connection* runs to Wellington in the morning, returning to Palmerston North in the evening (departs Palmerston North 6.20am, Wellington 5.17pm, journey time two hours). The train stops at each major station between Palmerston North and Paraparaumu, taking you through the lush Manawatu and the coastal settlements of the Kapiti Coast. Fare $19.50 one way, concessions available.

- **Wairarapa–Wellington:** see GETTING AROUND THE CITY.

Wellington Railway Station

The foundation stone of Wellington Railway Station was laid in 1934. The station opened three years later amid great jubilation, the acting prime minister deeming it 'worthy of Wellington and worthy of the capital city'. Public approval was immediate.

The station's architectural style can be loosely described as neo-Georgian. A Beaux Arts influence is evident in the large garden forecourt, and the grand frontage portico and Doric columns add a Roman element. Beyond the portico is a large Beaux Arts style barrel-vaulted booking hall with a coffered and arched ceiling. It is reminiscent of the Roman bathhouse, but perhaps the whole inspiration is drawn from the Pennsylvania Station in New York. Giving access to the trains, the main concourse is totally different in style, revealing a dual attitude to architecture in those days – decorative at the front, functional at the back.

The building is made of brick and concrete with a granite base and Spanish Mission tiles on the roof. On the facades, under the windows, are panels of purple, yellow and green ceramic tiles, softening the brick effect. Whangarei and Hanmer marbles are used extensively.

WELLINGTON RAILWAY STATION, BUNNY STREET

Station facilities include an onward travel ticket office, luggage lockers, kiosks and Trax Bar and Cafe.

For connections: the *Interisland Line* free shuttle and *Intercity* buses leave from platform 9; for *city bus services* including the *Stagecoach Flyer*, follow the walkway to 'City Centre and Surburban Buses'; the *city circular* bus leaves from the front entrance of the station. Taxis can also be found at the front.

Wellingtonians use public transport more than anyone else in New Zealand. About 26,000 people commute into the city every day. Twenty-eight percent of Wellingtonians use public transport to commute compared with 18% in Auckland, 9% in Christchurch and an average of 10% in Australian and North American cities. Walking to work is also very high by international standards at about 11%.

Coach

INTERCITY COACHLINES
Tel 472-5111, www.intercitycoach.co.nz
New Zealand's largest coach network covers 600 destinations
nationwide. A *Flexi-Pass* allows multiple journeys on the network;
enquire for details. The *Starlighter* is the overnight service between
Auckland and Wellington, leaving both cities at 7.50pm every
night, arriving at 6.50am. Seats are comfortable and there are
some facilities onboard. Departs/arrives Railway Station platform
9. Cost $67, special fares available.

KIWI TRAVELLER
Tel 0800-500-100, www.kiwitraveller.co.nz
Scheduled bus services between Wellington and Rotorua, stopping
everywhere in between including Palmerston North and Tongariro
National Park. Hop on and off as many times as you like along
the route in one direction. Tickets remain valid for six months,
so there's no need to rush. Backpacks, guitars and surfboards
enjoy safe stowage. Rotorua–Wellington Tues/Thurs/Sat 9am;
Wellington–Rotorua Mon/Wed/Fri 10.30am. Journey time eight
hours. Hostel pick-up/drop-off. Standard one-way Wellington–
Rotorua fare is $66, with deals and discounts available.

BAY XPRESS COACHLINES
Tel 0800-422-997, www.bayxpress.co.nz
Scheduled daily bus services between Wellington and Napier via
Palmerston North, 364 days a year. Tickets available from visitor
information centres or from the driver on the day of travel. Bikes,
surfboards and other items welcome. Departs Wellington from the
bus stop opposite the Duxton Hotel on Wakefield Street at 3pm and
Downtown Backpackers in Bunny Street at 3.05pm. Departs Napier
8am. Journey time five hours. Adult fare $35 one way.

For hassle-free, no-fee bookings for bus services, go and
see the staff at the *Wellington Visitor Information Centre*.

Car

There are two road routes into Wellington from the north. If you find yourself at the crossroads, here's a few highlights to help you choose your route.

Kapiti Route – SH1	Wairarapa Route – SH2
A coastal journey along the dramatic Kapiti coast.	The inland route through plains and quaint country towns.
Some traffic to contend with (try to avoid peak hours).	Lighter traffic flows, but a climb over the scenic Rimutaka Hill.
Views of the beautiful Tararuas to the east.	Views of the beautiful Tararuas to the west.
Otaki's Brown Sugar Café. Yum.	Try a homemade pie, anywhere.
Walk or picnic in the Tararuas via Otaki Forks.	Enjoy birds and bush at the Mt Bruce National Wildlife Centre.
Stop at the Lindale Centre for Kapiti cheese and other delights such as ice cream, honey, olives, café, art and farm tours.	Visit Carterton's paua shell factory, or browse antiques, arts, craft and boutique shopping throughout the region.
Visit QEII park for a picnic, swim or walk on the beach.	Detour to Martinborough wine country.
Shop till you drop at North City, Porirua – the region's latest shopping centre.	Shun the highway and dawdle through the leafy Hutt Valley with its many attractions.

Try a bit of both sides by crossing at either the *Akatarawa Road* (a leafy gorge) or *Paekakariki Hill* (spectacular views of the South Island).

Driving times to Wellington are approximately 12 hours from Whangarei; 9 hours from Auckland; 8 hours from Hamilton; 7 hours from Rotorua; 5 hours from Taupo, New Plymouth or Napier; 2 hours from Palmerston North; and 90 minutes from Masterton.

Speeding and parking fines: if you leave the country without paying them, they grow and greet you when you next visit.

Sea

The North and South Islands are separated by the 32 km **Cook Strait**, named after Captain James Cook, who entered it in 1770.

The first person to swim across the Strait was Barrie Devenport in 1962. It took him 11 hours, 13 minutes. In 1978, 16-year-old Meda McKenzie became the first person to swim it in both directions – but not at once. Philip Rush took that honour in 1984, his return crossing taking him 16 hours, 16 minutes. It was kayaked by Rob Martin, a double amputee, in April 2001 in 3½ hours.

Whatever your means, the Cook Strait crossing is a wonderful, often exciting journey. The cruise through the Marlborough Sounds is justifiably famous for its views, serenity and the opportunity to see dolphins frolicking and pleasure-craft cruising. Two companies offer services across the strait.

THE INTERISLAND LINE

Tel 0800-802-802, www.interislandline.co.nz
The Interisland Line operates a frequent ferry service for foot and vehicle passengers between Wellington and Picton. The Interisland Line's two conventional ferries – *Arahura* and *Aratere* – take three hours to cross the Strait. Alternatively, passengers can take the *Lynx* fast ferry that takes 2 hours, 15 minutes. Fares start from $30 per adult, $100 per car and $15 per child one-way. Note: the ferries and the Lynx depart from different places (see MAP 1). A free shuttle bus runs from the railway station (platform 9) to the ferry terminal, 35 minutes before every sailing. You can walk to the Lynx terminal from the city centre.

BLUEBRIDGE

Tel 0800-844-844, www.strait.co.nz
'The Cook Strait alternative' – established in 1992 to give Tranz Rail a run for their money, and reports are positive. There are two ferry sailings in each direction per day; cars can come too. The journey time is 3 hours, 20 minutes, and one-way fares are adult $40, cars around $110. You may find Bluebridge a cheaper option if you have a car, particularly during peak season. The terminal is next to the Lynx, a short walk from the city centre.

Getting Around the City

Getting around Wellington is easy and pleasant. The city is compact, there's relatively little congestion and few fumes. For many of us, our commute involves a stroll along the waterfront or a scoot down the hill. Public transport is simple to use, and locals will delight in giving you directions.

Exploring on Foot

Wellington is a wonderful city for walking, with many attractions scattered within a 30-minute-stroll radius. Don't be afraid to explore shortcuts – you can't get lost if you look for landmarks. Those endless steps and zig-zag paths will save you time and reward you with wonderful views. Walking Wellington is highly recommended. See CITY WALKS for inspiration.

Buses and Trains

The *Ridewell* transport information line, with real live people at the end of the phone, offers free city transport information including timetables, fares and connections.

> **Ridewell** tel 801-7000
> freephone 0800-801-700
> www.gw.govt.nz

The same people produce the useful *Bus & Train Guide* and a range of timetables available from the *Wellington Regional Council* at 142 Wakefield Street, or from the *Visitor Information Centre*, *Central Library* foyer, *City Stops* and *Star Marts*.

To catch a bus, look for a standard bus stop sign and wave to the driver as they approach. Pay the driver as you enter; exact fare is appreciated but small notes can usually be changed. If you don't know where to get off, ask the driver to let you off at the closest stop to your destination, otherwise press the buzzer when you get close to where you want to go.

There are several **day passes** available after 9am Mon–Fri, and any time Sat/Sun and public holidays: the *Capital Explorer Pass* ($15) offers unlimited travel on train or bus for one full day anywhere within the Wellington region (except Wairarapa), the *Discovery Pass* ($10) is the same but for bus services only, the *Star Pass* ($8) offers bus-only services as far as Upper Hutt, and the *Day Tripper* ticket ($5) allows bus-only services as far as Ngauranga Gorge.

Stagecoach operates city and suburban bus services to nearly every corner of the city, with its city interchanges at the railway station and Courtenay Place. There's only one major route through the city centre, so you won't wait long. Inner city tickets are $1. Further destinations are divided into fare sections, the maximum fare $3.50. Timetables are displayed at bus stops.

The **Stagecoach Flyer** runs from *Wellington airport* to *Upper Hutt*, stopping at Hataitai, Kilbirnie, Rongotai, all city stops to Molesworth Street, then Petone, Alicetown, Lower Hutt, Taita, Stokes Valley, Silverstream, Barton Road, Moonshine Road and Upper Hutt. Look for the bright orange signs at bus stops. Services operate Mon–Fri at approximately 30-minute intervals 6.20am–8.20pm; Sat/Sun hourly 6.50am–8.50am, at 30-minutes from 9.50am–6.50pm, and hourly again 6.50pm–8.50pm. Fares adult $2–$11, child $1–$5.50.

Cityline offers bus services from the city to *Petone*, *Hutt Valley* and *Eastbourne*. The Eastbourne bus (no. 83, $5) runs every half hour or so from the city, but catching the ferry is more fun (see below).

Newlands, *Johnsonville*, and *Porirua* are served by **Newlands & Mana Coach Services** – ring *Ridewell* for connections, fares and timetables.

There are train services between Wellington and *Johnsonville*, *Paraparaumu*, the *Hutt Valley* and *Masterton* run by **Tranz Metro** (www.tranzmetro.co.nz). The Masterton service runs several times per day Mon–Fri, and twice daily on weekends. The journey takes you through the second longest railway tunnel in New Zealand – 8798 metres to be precise! The wonderful Wairarapa makes a great day trip from the capital. Fares are $2–$13 per adult one way.

There are two options to *Wainuiomata*. Take the **Tranz Metro** train to Waterloo and catch the connecting bus, or take the no. 83 or 91 bus to Lower Hutt Queensgate, and catch the connecting bus. Purchase a Stagecoach Star Pass and a return journey will cost $8.

TRAVEL & TRANSPORT

Dominion Post Ferry

Queens Wharf, tel 499-1282, www.eastbywest.co.nz
Explore Matiu/Somes Island or Eastbourne on the city's harbour
ferry service. Up to nine return sailings daily between Queens
Wharf, Matiu/Somes and Eastbourne's Days Bay, with a journey
time of 20–30 minutes. A licensed bar offers refreshments including
beer, snacks and ice cream. A one-way adult fare is $7.50. Telephone
494-3339 for up-to-date timetable information.

Wellington Cable Car

For some lucky locals, this is commuting. For the rest of us, it's an
adventure – see CITY LOOKOUTS.

Taxi

There are numerous taxi companies in Wellington, with *Wellington
Combined Taxis* being the favourite amongst women travelling alone
(tel 384-4444). There are taxi stands throughout the city.

Rental Car

The **Yellow Pages** (www.yellowpages.co.nz) has extensive rental
car listings, featuring the usual worldwide companies, and some
inexpensive local operators (from around $25 per day).

Scooter

Scootour (70 Abel Smith Street, tel 384-7679, www.scootour.co.nz)
offer scooter rental by the hour, with only a car licence (and some
skill) required. For the over 18s only. Map and a full fuel tank
provided. Not for motorway use, and other conditions apply. Guided
tours by arrangement. *Open* Mon–Sun from 8am. Rental is $25 for the
first hour, $7 per hour thereafter, full day $60.

Car Parking

A combination of coin meters and pay-and-display parking are
available street-side throughout the city. Most offer a two-hour
limit, although there are the odd 30- or 60-minute limits in places.
City centre charges are generally $3 per hour.

The city centre has lots of **car parking buildings**, many open 24 hours a day. Charges vary, but expect to pay up to $6 per hour.

You'll find **coupon parking** areas on the margins of the city centre. Look for the signs to see if you are in a coupon zone. The first two hours are free, but you need a coupon to stay longer. Coupons are readily available for $4 from dairies and garages, allowing you to stay all day. Display as per instructions.

All public on-street parking is **free at weekends** (although this may change in 2004, so double check).

Residents Only parking zones are clearly marked. Spare a thought for the residents and don't park there.

For those in a **campervan**, your best bet is the *Te Papa* car park.

TRAVEL & TRANSPORT

Bypass or not to Bypass

Since the 1960s, Wellingtonians have debated whether a proposed motorway extension should be allowed to pass through the inner city.

The 'bypass', as it's known, would cut a 700-metre-long swathe through upper Willis and Cuba Streets, providing a corridor to ease congestion and speed up traffic flows to and from Wellington's eastern suburbs, hospital and airport. *Transit New Zealand*, responsible for New Zealand's highways, says the bypass will also provide a safer route for pedestrians and cyclists, as well as reduce pollution and facilitate improved public transport systems. Some local people welcome the development: 'I walk or cycle through this area every day, and I'd be glad to have less traffic to contend with,' says one.

The bypass has, however, met with persistent and at times forceful protest, and its opponents present compelling arguments. The proposed corridor is home to some of the oldest wooden cottages in central Wellington (particulary the Cuba Street and Tonks Avenue junction). While many inner city heritage buildings have already been cleared to make way for modern commercial premises and apartment complexes, the area under threat affords a unique glimpse into Wellington City's colonial era. And although a number of these buildings will be moved and preserved, opponents say that too much will still be lost, not least of all the artistic and somewhat counter-culture community that has long been part of the neighbourhood.

Bypass opponents also argue that the alleged journey-time savings will be less than currently claimed, while congestion will simply be transferred to another part of town. Lobby groups such as *Campaign for a Better City* believe that other solutions should be sought, such as encouraging the use of public transport.

As this book goes to print, the debate rages on and the bypass is stalled. Local residents and small businesses cling on, awaiting their fate, while the rickety old buildings deteriorate with the passing years. In fact, some would argue that the reason the area has maintained its frayed charm in the face of rampant development in adjoining areas is actually because of the proposed bypass: *Transit* now owns much of the property on the route, and leaves it pretty much untouched in anticipation of knocking it down or moving it when the road works finally begin. So for now, you can still see what the fuss is all about. But be quick … it looks as if the bypass will go ahead – as to when that will be is not known for sure.

For more information, visit
Transit New Zealand, **www.transit.govt.nz/innercitybypass**
Campaign for a Better City, **www.cbc.org.nz**

Positively Wellington Tourism (Nick Servian)

Useful Information

Information Centres and Services

New Zealand's *Visitor Information Network* provides local and national tourist information, as well as a no-fee booking service for transport and accommodation.

Wellington Visitor Information Centre
Corner Victoria & Wakefield Streets (Civic Square), Wellington, tel 802-4860, **www.wellingtonnz.com**, email bookings@wellingtonnz.com

Wellington Airport Visitor Information Centre
First floor, Main Terminal, tel 385-5123

Hutt City Visitor Information Centre
10 Andrews Avenue, Lower Hutt, tel 560-4715, **www.huttcityinfo.co.nz**

Upper Hutt Visitor Information Centre
6 Main Street, Upper Hutt, tel 527-2141, **www.upperhuttcity.com**

Porirua Visitor Information Centre
8 Cobham Court, Porirua, tel 237-8088, **www.discoverporirua.co.nz**

USEFUL INFORMATION

Paraparaumu Visitor Information Centre

Coastlands Carpark, SH1, Paraparaumu, tel (04) 298-8195, www.kapititourist.co.nz

Kapiti Coast Visitor Information Centre

Centennial Park, SH1, Otaki, tel (06) 364-7620, www.kapititourist.co.nz

Masterton Visitor Information Centre

Transit Building, Queen Street, Masterton, tel (06) 377-7577, www.wairarapanz.com

Martinborough Visitor Information Centre

18 Kitchener Street, Martinborough, tel (06) 306-9043, www.wairarapanz.com

Featherston Visitor Information Centre

The Old Courthouse, SH2, Featherston, tel (06) 308-8051, www.wairarapanz.com

DEPARTMENT OF CONSERVATION (DOC) OFFICE

Government Buildings, Lambton Quay (opposite the Beehive), tel 472-7356, www.doc.govt.nz

Provides information about national parks, forest parks and scenic reserves. Brochures, maps, hut passes, permits and general conservation information available.

WELLINGTON CITY COUNCIL

101 Wakefield Street, tel 499-4444, www.wellington.govt.nz

On the Wellington City Council webiste you can find information about everything from rates to the community directory to how to apply for a bar manager's licence. Whether you want to read the latest Council news or find out where your nearest recycling station is located, their website is the place to do it.

GREATER WELLINGTON REGIONAL COUNCIL

142 Wakefield Street, tel 384-5708, www.gw.govt.nz

See Greater Wellington Regional Council for brochures or other information on the five regional parks and the Akatarawa and Pakuratahi Forests. It is also the main point of contact for bus and train services in the region, from Otaki on the Kapiti Coast and Mt Bruce in the Wairarapa southwards to Cook Strait.

Accommodation

Wellington has a wide variety of accommodation, from five-star hotels to mid range motels, bed and breakfasts, and budget backpackers. Most are within walking distance of the city, although campers and motorhome travellers will have to look further afield.

It pays to book in advance during the busy season – November to March. And watch out if there's a big game on at the stadium – it can be hard to find a room. Weekend deals and other offers are available, so be sure to ask.

The *Wellington Visitor Information Centre* (tel 802-4860) can help with bookings and special deals; useful listings can be found on their website, **www.wellingtonnz.com** – follow the *accommodation* link.

Tourism New Zealand's website is also useful for listings across all budgets, all over the country. Visit **www.purenz.com** and follow the *places to stay* link.

The online *Yellow Pages* are also handy, **www.yellowpages.co.nz** – search under *accommodation & Wellington*.

For extensive listings across all types of accommodation, try **www.aaguides.co.nz**, the accommodation site of the *Automobile Association*. They also produce a book of the same, $12 from bookshops or free to AA members from AA offices.

There are plenty of *backpacker* hostels in the $18–$45 per person price range. For listings, pick up the *BBH* booklet, or visit **www.backpack.co.nz**. The *YHA* on Wakefield Street (tel 801-7280) is the closest hostel to Te Papa, and the *Cambridge Backpackers* (tel 385-8829) is not far away either. If you want to be near the Railway Station, try *Downtown Backpackers* (tel 473-8482).

Bed and breakfast (or *homestay*) accommodation is good value and a wonderful way to experience Kiwi hospitality. There are over 50 hosts in Wellington, most of which are listed at **www.bnb.co.nz** – an easy to use online version of the bestselling *New Zealand Bed & Breakfast Book* ($19.95 at bookshops). Prices range from $55–$250 per person per night.

There are many mid range *hotels* and *motor inns* for families and budget-conscious visitors. Centrally located in Cuba Street is

The Chancellor (tel 385-2153, formerly Trekkers), around $130 for a double. Popular family options include **Harbour City** (tel 384-9809) and **Carillon** (tel 384-8795) – both within a short walk of Civic Square. A family suite will cost from $100 per room per night.

Lodges offer good value accommodation with options to suit all needs. Consistent performers are **Halswell Lodge** (tel 385-0196), **Tinakori Lodge** (tel 939-3478) and **Ruby House** (tel 934-7930).

Serviced apartments abound. **City Life** (tel 0800-2489-5433) and **Central City** (tel 0800-804-255) both offer family suites – a two bedroom unit will cost around $160–$260 per night; some special deals available.

At the plusher end of the scale you'll find the 'hotel de wheels' **Museum Hotel** (tel 802-8900) opposite Te Papa and competitively priced, and **The Duxton** (tel 473-3900) on Wakefield Street stands out for its excellent restaurant. **The Wellesley Hotel** (tel 473-1308) is the place to stay if you like character and class.

Campervan and motorhome travellers – the closest park to town is the **Top 10 Hutt Park Holiday Park** (95 Hutt Park Road, Lower Hutt, tel 568-5914, www.huttpark.co.nz) with 91 power and plenty of tent sites. There are more camping sites further afield including non-powered DOC sites for adventurers. For more information, refer to Kerr & Hansen's handy **New Zealand Camping Guide** (bookshops, $16.95).

Stay with a friend! If you haven't got one, make one, and be assured of splendid meals, great company and lots of help having fun.

Public Holidays

	2004	2005
New Years Day	1 January	3 January
New Years Holiday	2 January	4 January
Wellington Anniversary	19 January	24 January
Waitangi Day	6 February	6 February
Good Friday	9 April	25 March
Easter Monday	12 April	28 March
Anzac Day	25 April	25 April
Queen's Birthday	7 June	6 June
Labour Day	25 October	24 October
Christmas Day Holiday	27 December	26 December
Boxing Day Holiday	28 December	27 December

Events Calendar

Here are some highlights of the Wellington year. For all the
rest and up-to-date details, visit **www.feelinggreat.co.nz** or
www.wellingtonnz.com, or just keep your eyes peeled.

JANUARY

Summer City
www.feelinggreat.co.nz
More than 60 free outdoor events courtesy of Wellington City Council.
Concerts, picnics and wonderful Whopper Choppers. *31 Dec–29 Feb.*

More FM Beach Volleyball Pro Tour
www.beachvolleyballnz.org.nz
Oriental Bay beach sees barefooted two-person teams battling it out
as part of the national volleyball tour. *10–11 Jan.*

Wonderland
www.heloid.org
A 'nice party' and quite possibly the best outdoor dance music event
in New Zealand. *17 Jan.*

Wellington Cup Week
www.trentham.co.nz
Horse racing. The highlight of the week is *Wellington Cup Day*
– fashion, entertainment and exciting racing. High stakes and the
best horses and jockeys available. *17–24 Jan.*

Organic River Festival
www.ecofest.co.nz
A weekend of organic feasting, family fun and live music in an
idyllic Levin location. *17–19 Jan.*

Pinot Noir 2004
www.pinotnoir2004.co.nz
An opportunity to meet international winemakers and sample their
products; street party and public tastings. *28–31 Jan.*

National Downhill Mountain Bike Championships
www.mountainbike.co.nz
Downhill fast, where no sane person would normally go. *31 Jan–1 Feb.*

FEBRUARY

One Love 2004
www.radioactive.fm
The city's annual celebration of Bob Marley's birthday, happily coinciding with Waitangi Day. Music and family fun in the Velodrome at Hataitai Park. Bring a picnic and sunscreen. *6 Feb.*

New Zealand International Sevens Tournament
www.sevens.co.nz
Sixteen of the world's top seven-a-side rugby teams compete at the Westpac Stadium. Fast, energetic and popular, so book early. *6–7 Feb.*

Line 7 Port Nicholson Regatta
www.rpnyc.org.nz
Yacht racing in the harbour, incorporating the national club and Flying Dutchman championships, international youth match racing and open keelboat divisions. *18–22 Feb.*

Fringe New Zealand Festival
www.fringe.org.nz
Live theatre, comedy, poetry, visual arts, dance, music and more – the Fringe Festival sets the streets alive and keeps the city buzzing day and night. *14 Feb–14 Mar.*

Cuba Street Carnival
www.cubacarnival.org.nz
A vibrant, global mix of music, dance and cultural diversity; Aotearoa's largest free street festival. *27–29 Feb.*

Round the Bays Fun-Run-Walk
www.sportwellington.org.nz
An annual community fundraiser involving thousands of runners and walkers. Entertainment, refreshments, massage and spot prizes.

New Zealand International Arts Festival
www.nzfestival.telecom.co.nz
Rapidly developing a reputation as one of the finest cultural showpieces in the world. Classical music, jazz, pop, opera, dance, puppetry, poetry and experimental performance. Something for every taste. Biennial. *27 Feb–21 Mar.*

MARCH

Wellington Dragon Boat Festival
www.dragonboat.org.nz
Up to 60,000 people converge on the waterfront to enjoy the atmosphere as thousands of paddlers thrash it out on the water. Colourful community fun. *6–7 Mar.*

Gay and Lesbian Fair
An annual institution for nearly 20 years, this celebration is light-hearted and lots of fun. Loads of stalls and entertainment. Held at Newtown School.

Red Bull Flugtag Festival
www.redbullflugtag.co.nz
'You'll laugh. You'll fly. Just not very far.' Yes folks, it's the one where crazy people throw themselves off Taranaki Street Wharf with homemade wings – 'designed by amateurs, built by volunteers, piloted by madmen'. We can't wait for this one! *14 Mar.*

APRIL

Super 12 Rugby
www.hurricanes.co.nz
The Westpac Stadium, home of the Hurricanes, hosts Super 12 matches during the Feb–May season. A chance to see just how good Tana Umaga really is! See website for fixtures and ticketing.

MAY

TV2 International Laugh! Festival
www.laugh.co.nz
A wide range of quality comedy staged all over town. International and national acts.

Monteiths Wild Food Challenge
www.monteiths.co.nz
Restaurants around Wellington (and nationwide) accept the challenge to create new wild food menus matched with Monteiths beers. The public help to select the winners.

JUNE

BrewNZ
www.brewnz.co.nz
A five-day celebration of brewing and great beer. Bringing together the nation's brewers and those who appreciate their talents.

The Food Show
www.foodshow.co.nz
An event for those with a passionate for food and drink.

Young and Hungry
www.youngandhungry.org.nz
BATS Theatre and the *Young & Hungry Arts Trust* present a series of one act plays designed to give young people, aged between 15–25 years old, the opportunity to work in a professional theatre environment under the direction of professional theatre practitioners.

JULY

Wellington International Film Festival
www.enzedff.co.nz
Three weeks of movie-lovers madness with offerings from home and abroad. For other film festivals, see CINEMA.

AUGUST

NPC Rugby
www.wellingtonrugby.co.nz
The Westpac Stadium hosts NPC matches as visiting teams meet the Wellington Lions for the championship. The season runs August–October. Check the website for fixtures and ticketing.

SEPTEMBER

Wellington Fashion Festival
www.wellingtonfashionfestival.co.nz
An annual showcase of the hippest, funkiest and most glamorous fashions. Local and national designers launch their spring and summer collections at events throughout the city.

Dance Your Socks Off!
www.feelinggreat.co.nz
Wellington's annual celebration of dance, with amazing performances, films, classes and workshops – for everyone.

OCTOBER

Wellington International Jazz Festival
www.jazzfestival.co.nz
A citywide, quality musical adventure including international acts, jazz on the streets and jazz on the waterfront.

Asia 2000 Diwali – Festival of Lights
www.feelinggreat.co.nz
Celebrate Indian culture with a traditional festival in the city centre. Scrumptious food, non-stop free family entertainment, Bollywood dancing, traditional crafts and much more.

NOVEMBER

Dunlop Targa New Zealand
www.targa.co.nz
Classic cars meet contemporary in New Zealand's biggest road race.

Toast Martinborough
www.toastmartinborough.co.nz
One of New Zealand's best wine, food and music events, set in the vineyards of Martinborough. Book early for tickets.

DECEMBER

Carols by Candlelight
www.feelinggreat.co.nz
Thousands of Wellingtonians join together for a night of singing and dancing in the heart of the city.

See more! Do more!
For film festivals, see CINEMA.
For ballet, opera and concerts, see DRAMA, DANCE AND CONCERTS.
For more sports fixtures, see SPECTATOR SPORTS.

USEFUL INFORMATION

Newspapers, Magazines and Radio

Dependable newsagents for local and international material are *Magnetix* on Midland Park, Lambton Quay, and *George Soteros* near the corner of Victoria & Manners Streets (family owned for 70 years).

The *Dominion Post* is Wellington's daily paper (no Sunday edition). The best days for entertainment listings are Thursday and Saturday; job listings Wednesday and Saturday. Auckland's *New Zealand Herald* and the *Christchurch Press*, from newsagents, provide comparable reading. For online news try **www.nzoom.com** or **www.stuff.co.nz**.

The *Capital Times* is an easy-to-find free weekly local paper, out on Wednesday. Useful in many ways, it includes comprehensive entertainment listings and reviews, interesting articles and neighbourhood gossip.

The *Package*, free weekly and also easy to find, is a terrific little guide to what's on in Wellington (and beyond) with a focus on live music and exhibitions. *Pulp freetime* is similar, snazzy, free monthly, with more articles and advertising.

Up is Wellington's gay newspaper, and the only free gay monthly in New Zealand. Find it at newsagents, *Unity Books*, *Pound* nightclub and many cafés.

Radio Stations

Radio Active 89FM – independent, loads of Kiwi music, we love it
Channel Z 91.7/94.7FM – the best in alternative and popular
Concert 92.5/95.6AM – classics, jazz and opera, commercial free
National Radio 567AM – informing and entertaining, commercial free
Firm 107FM – solid dance music, 24 hours a day
91ZM 90.9/93.5FM – breakfast banter and pop hits
Access Radio 783AM – the voice of the Wellington community
Atiawa Toa 94.9/96.9FM – the soul selection
Radio Pacific 711AM – talkback, horse racing, insomniacs
Radio Sport 1535AM – live commentary, news and discussion
Newstalk ZB 89.4FM – news, talkback, lifestyle
More FM 98.9/100FM – more hit music
The Breeze 94/98AM – easy listening
Classic Hits 90FM – classic hits

Post, Telephone and Email

New Zealand Post shops (**www.nzpost.com**) are located all over town, open Mon–Fri 9am–5pm. The *Manners Street Post Office* (which holds **Poste Restante**) is open Saturday until 1pm. Postage stamps are also available from some newsagents and bookshops. A postcard to anywhere in the world requires a $1.50 stamp.

Public telephone booths operate mostly on Telecom cards (usual outlets), although a few still accept coins. Credit cards and long-distance calling cards usually accepted as well. Useful operator numbers are: 010 national operator, 018 national directory services, 0170 international operator; and 0172 international directory services.

The **telephone code** for Wellington is 04 – and while you don't need to use it in the city, you do need to dial it for Kapiti numbers – that's north of Paekakariki to just south of Otaki. Any 0800 number is free. To make *international calls*, dial 00 before the country code.

You'll need to check with your **mobile phone** provider regarding roaming facilities. New Zealand's networks providers are *Telecom* and *Vodafone*, with outlets around town.

Email and Internet access is available conveniently at *The Email Shop* at the Visitor Information Centre, Civic Square – charges are $4 per hour (they can do digital camera download to CD, and printing). There are several Internet cafes/providers dotted about too.

Money

Bank opening hours are Mon–Fri 9.30am–4.30pm, most offering **bureaux de change** at competitive rates. Getting currency exchange at the weekend is a challenge. We suggest you try either *Thomas Cook* at 358 Lambton Quay (Saturday mornings only), *Travelex* at the airport or the 24-hour *City Stop* at 107 Manners Street.

Tipping, while not essential, is an appropriate acknowledgement of good service and therefore encouraged. Don't be surprised, however, if your taxi driver chases you to give you change.

Duty-free shopping can be found at *Red Lane* (corner Willis & Mercer Streets) and at *Duty Free Stores*, Wellington airport landside and airside. Many other stores offer duty free goods, so do ask.

USEFUL INFORMATION

Emergency, Medical and Other Assistance

Dial **111** for emergencies – fire, police, ambulance.

The Wellington Central **Police Station** is next to the central library (corner Victoria & Harris Streets). Report crimes here, claim your lost property, or turn yourself in.

For minor ailments, a local doctor will see you for around $40. Two central city clinics are *City GPs* (189 Willis Street, tel 381-6161) and *Courtney Medical Centre* (corner Courtenay Place & Allen Street, tel 801-5228). See also *Yellow Pages*, 'medical clinics'.

ACCIDENT AND EMERGENCY SERVICES
Wellington Hospital, Riddiford Street, Newtown, tel 385-5999
Hutt Hospital, High Street, Lower Hutt, tel 566-6999
Kenepuru Hospital, Raiha Street, Porirua, tel 237-0179

AFTER-HOURS MEDICAL SERVICES AND PHARMACIES
17 Adelaide Road, Newtown, tel 384-4944
729 High Street, Lower Hutt, tel 567-5345
12-14 Royal Street, Upper Hutt, tel 528-0111
6 Hartham Place South, Porirua, tel 237-6777
Open: Medical services Mon–Fri 5pm–8am; weekends and public holidays, 24 hours; *Pharmacies* Mon–Fri 5pm–11pm; weekends and public holidays, 9am–11pm.

FAMILY PLANNING ASSOCIATION
Level 6, 35 Victoria Street, tel 499-1992
29 Waterloo Road, Lower Hut, tel 569-5025
1 Hartham Place South, Porirua, tel 237-8895
Sexual and reproductive health clinics, for contraception, STDs, pregnancy testing and the morning-after pill (now also available at pharmacies). New Zealand, UK and Australian residents pay $40 for a 15-minute appointment, other nationalities $60. Appointments required. *Open* Mon–Fri 8.30am–5.30pm (Wed 6.30pm close) Sat 9am–12pm. For emergencies tel 499-1992.

The Travel Doctor (Grand Arcade, Willis Street, tel 473-0991) provide vaccinations and stock a range of travel/health accessories.

Embassies and Consular Services

Those embassies and high commissions located in Wellington are listed below. For others, call in at the *Wellington Visitor Information Centre* to view their Diplomatic and Consular List, or search online at the Ministry of Foreign Affairs and Trade website, **www.mfat.govt.nz** (follow 'overseas representatives' link).

Australia, 72–78 Hobson Street, tel 473-6411

Brazil, 10 Brandon Street, tel 473-3516

Canada, 61 Molesworth Street, tel 473–9577

Chile, 19 Bolton Street, tel 471-6270

France, 34–42 Manners Street, tel 384-2555

Germany, 90–92 Hobson Street, tel 473-6063

Greece, 5–7 Willeston Street, tel 473-7775

Indonesia, 70 Glen Road, Kelburn, tel 475-8699

Iran, 151 Te Anau Road, Roseneath, tel 386-2976

Italy, 34 Grant Road, Thorndon, tel 473-5339

Japan, 18th Floor, Majestic Centre, 100 Willis Street, tel 473-1540

Korea, 11th Floor, ASB Bank Tower, 2 Hunter Street, tel 473-9073

Mexico, 111–115 Customhouse Quay, tel 472-0555

Netherlands, 10th Floor, Investment House, Cnr Featherston & Ballance Streets, tel 471-6390

Peru, Level 8, Cigna House, 40 Mercer Street, tel 499-8087

Philippines, 50 Hobson Street, Thorndon, tel 472-9848

Poland, 17 Upland Road, Kelburn, tel 475-9453

Switzerland, 22 Panama Street, tel 472-1593

United Kingdom, 44 Hill Street, Thorndon, tel 924-2888

United States of America, 29 Fitzherbert Terrace, Thorndon, tel 462-6000

USEFUL INFORMATION

Index

Map 1

Civic Square

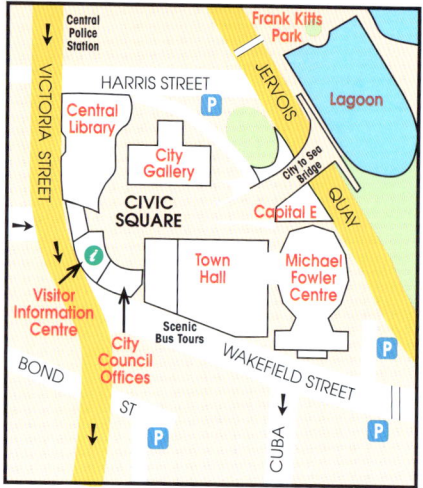

Central Police Station

HARRIS STREET

VICTORIA STREET

Central Library

City Gallery

CIVIC SQUARE

Visitor Information Centre

City Council Offices

BOND

ST

Scenic Bus Tours

Town Hall

Michael Fowler Centre

Capital E

City to Sea Bridge

JERVOIS

QUAY

Frank Kitts Park

Lagoon

WAKEFIELD STREET

CUBA

Ferry access routes

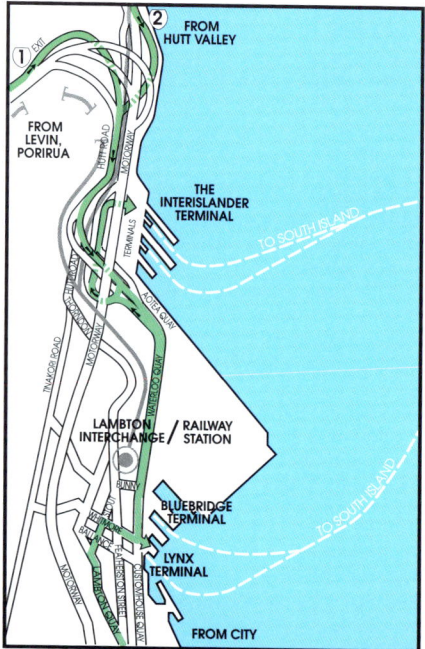

FROM HUTT VALLEY

1 EXIT

2

FROM LEVIN, PORIRUA

THE INTERISLANDER TERMINAL

TO SOUTH ISLAND

LAMBTON INTERCHANGE

RAILWAY STATION

BLUEBRIDGE TERMINAL

LYNX TERMINAL

TO SOUTH ISLAND

FROM CITY

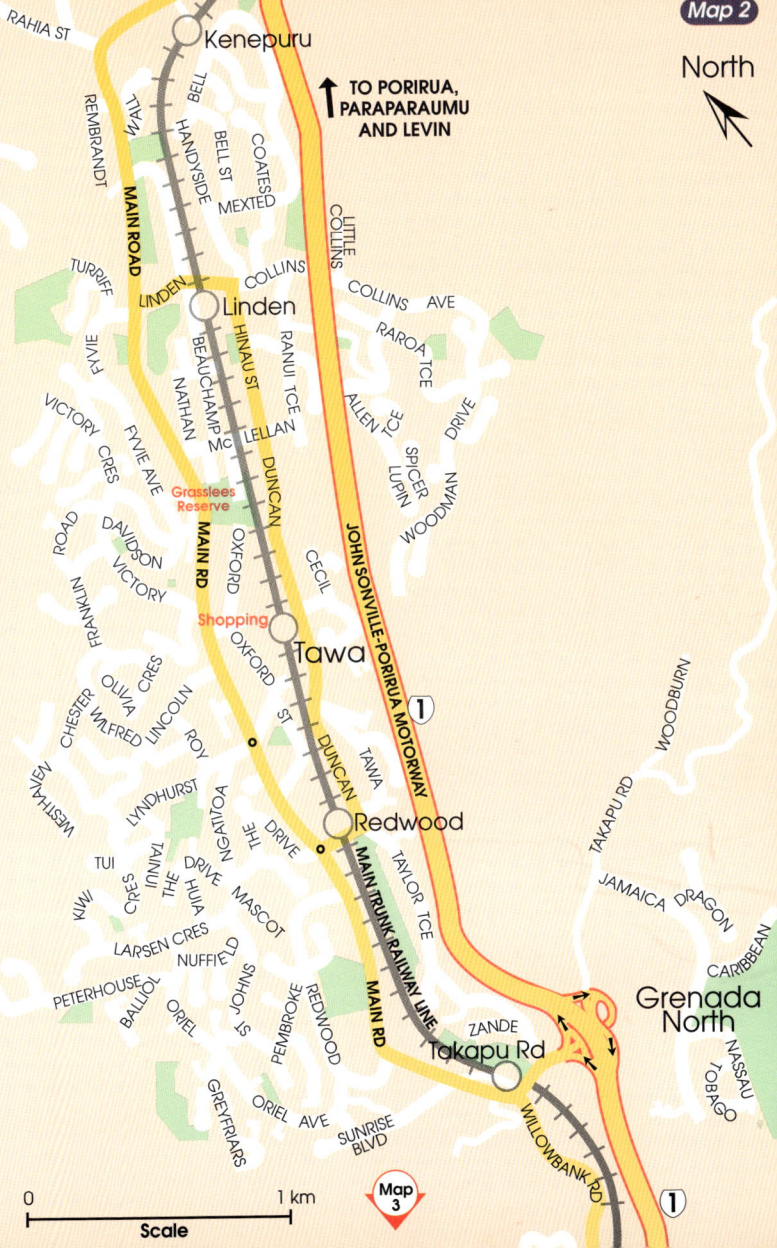

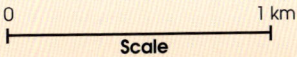

Map 3

TO TAWA, PORIRUA AND PARAPARAUMU

Map 2 Grenada Village

North

0 1 km
Scale

Glenside

Churton Park

Paparangi

Newlands

Johnsonville

Keith Spry Pool

Frankmoore

Raroa

Broadmeadows

Khandallah Park

Ngauranga

TO HUTT VALLEY

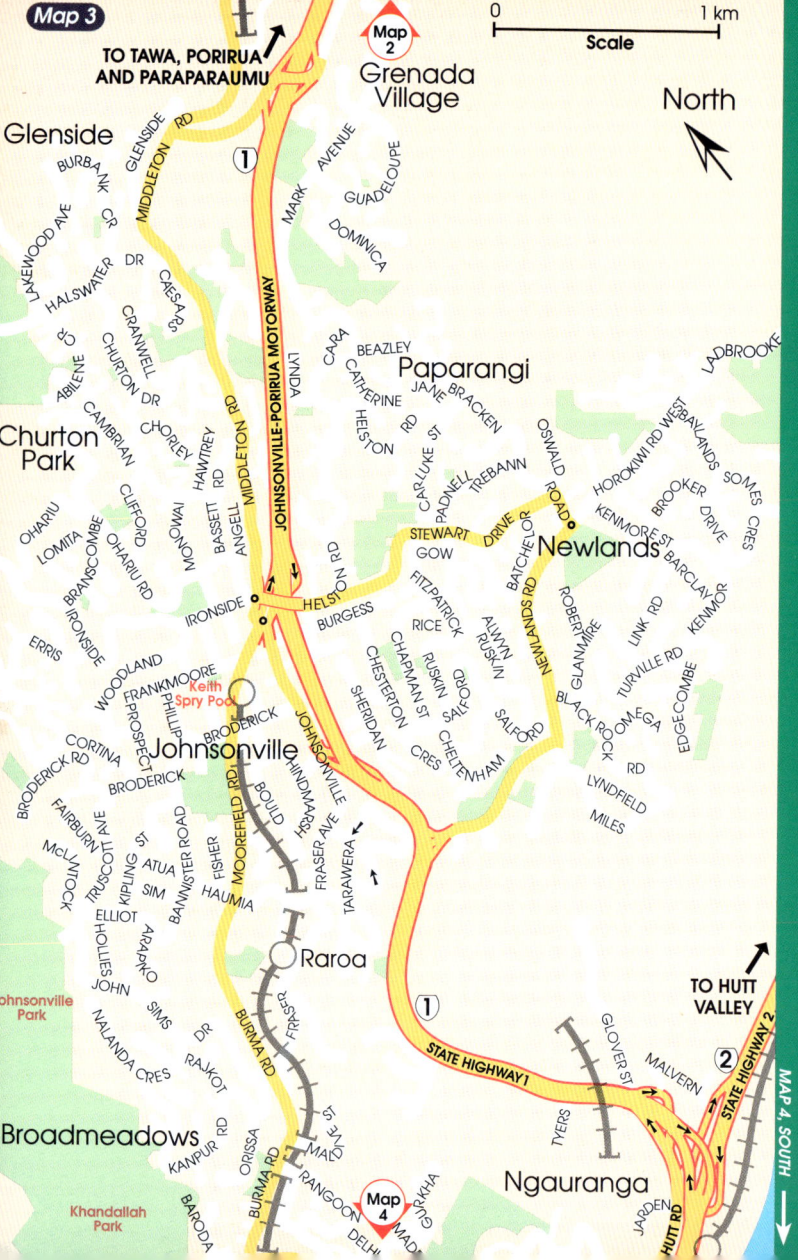

Map 4

MAP 4, SOUTH

STATE HIGHWAY 2

STATE HIGHWAY 1

JOHNSONVILLE–PORIRUA MOTORWAY

MIDDLETON RD

GLENSIDE RD

HELSTON RD

NEWLANDS RD

BATCHELOR RD

BURMA RD

HUTT RD

ohnsonville Park

Ladbrooke

Map 4

Khandallah Park

Map 3

STATION

Khandallah

WOODMANCOTE

BOX HILL

CLARK ST

CASHMERE

AVENUE

Box Hill

Shopping

CRES

SIMLA

LOCHIEL

AGRA

DEKKA

GANGES

EVEREST

IZARD

AMRITSAR

LOHIA ST

ONSLOW

ROAD

SATARA

AMAPUR

DR

SIMLA

Simla
Cres

CLUTHA

TORWOOD

NICHOLSON

JUBILEE

CLIVE

1

2

GAYA GR

FOX ST

KANDY

NGATOTO

Nairnville
Park

CALCUTTA

BENGAL

RAMA

AWARUA

STREET

IWI

ROTHSAY

KHANDALLAH

MYSORE

WARU

WHITU

RANGIORA

KARA MU

CHELMSFORD

ST

COLWAY ST

BOMBAY

COCKAYNE RD

PUNJAB

HUTT RD

MOJEKA

ST

ABBOTT

RD

KABUL

Kaiwharawhara

HEKE

HEKE

ST

OTTAWA

CROFTON

COCKAYNE

OLD PORIRUA RD

KAIWHARAWHARA RD

Ngaio

KENYA

PERTH

Ngaio Gorge Rd

ANNE

BARNARD

SARIST

URBAN MOTORWAY

Interislander
Ferry Terminal

Crofton
Downs

Shopping

JOHNSONVILLE RAILWAY LINE

HANOVER

FERNHILL

PITT ST

OBAN ST

SEFTON ST

WELLINGTON

SPENCER

CHURCHILL

WADESTOWN

RANKIN

PITT

WADESTOWN

HUTT RD

AOTEA QUAY

WINSTON

BLACKBRIDGE

ROAD

RAWELL

WADE

ROAD

WELD

Wadestown

Katherine
Mansfield
Birthplace

Westpac
Stadium

WATERLOO QUAY

DOWNING

CHARTWELL

CHURCHILL DR

ROSE

CECIL RD

THORNDON QUAY

HOBSON

WILTON BUSH

WILTON

MILTON

MAIRANGI

THORNDON QUAY

MURPHY

MULGRAVE

Pipitea

Otari –
Wilton's
Bush

ROAD

STREET

EUSTON

EDGEWARE

CECIL

RD

PARK

TINAKORI

Wellington
Railway Station
Lambton
Interchange

WARWICK

MAIRANGI RD

Town
Belt

Thorndon

HAWKESTONE

MOLESWORTH

HILL

Wilton

ROCHESTER

PEMBROKE

HUNTINGDON

TINAKORI RD

HILL ST

Parliament
Buildings

BOWEN

LAMBTON

THE TERRACE

FEATHERSTON ST

CUSTOMHOUSE

Map 5

WILTON RD

WORCESTER

PEMBROKE

CHESHIRE

BEDFORD

ORANGI KAUI

Map 6

BOLTON

See City
Centre Map

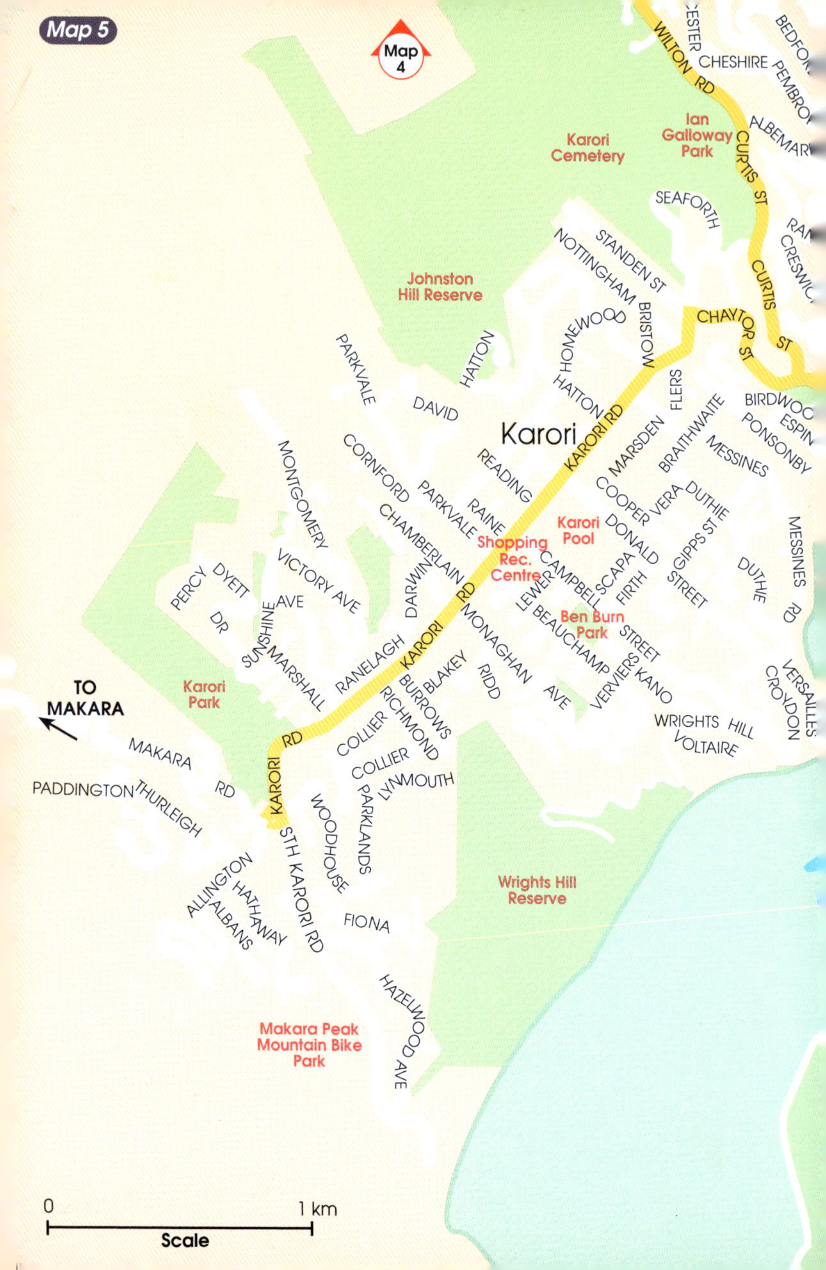
Map 5
Map 4
TO MAKARA
Karori
Karori Cemetery
Ian Galloway Park
Johnston Hill Reserve
Karori Pool
Shopping
Rec. Centre
Ben Burn Park
Karori Park
Wrights Hill Reserve
Makara Peak Mountain Bike Park
WILTON RD
CHESHIRE
BEDFOR
PEMBROK
ALBEMAR
CURTIS ST
SEAFORTH
STANDEN ST
NOTTINGHAM
BRISTOW
HOMEWOOD
CHAYTOR ST
HATTON
PARKVALE
DAVID
KARORI RD
MARSDEN
FLERS
BRAITHWAITE
BIRDWOOD
ESPIN
PONSONBY
MESSINES
READING
CORNFORD
MONTGOMERY
PARKVALE
RAINE
COOPER
VERA
DUTHIE
DONALD
GIPPS ST
CHAMBERLAIN
CAMPBELL
SCAPA
FIRTH
STREET
VICTORY AVE
PERCY
DYETT
DR
SUNSHINE AVE
DARWIN
LEWER
BEAUCHAMP
MESSINES RD
DUTHIE
MARSHALL
RANELAGH
MONAGHAN AVE
BLAKEY
RIDD
VERVIERS
KANO
STREET
BURROWS
RICHMOND
COLLIER
VERSAILLES
CROYDON
WRIGHTS HILL
VOLTAIRE
MAKARA RD
PADDINGTON
THURLEIGH
LYNMOUTH
PARKLANDS
WOODHOUSE
STH KARORI RD
ALLINGTON
HATHAWAY
ALBANS
FIONA
HAZELWOOD AVE
0
1 km
Scale

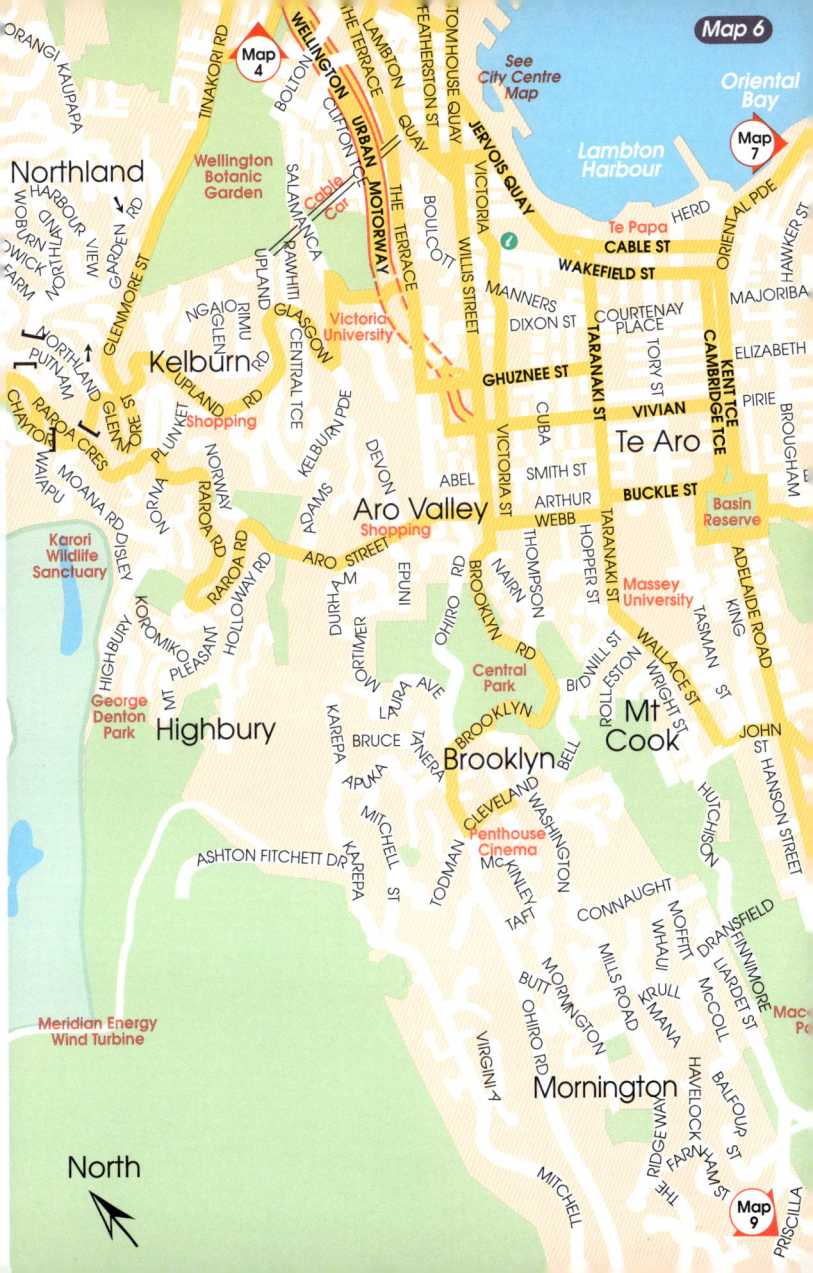

Map 6

Map 4

WELLINGTON

Map 7

Oriental Bay

See City Centre Map

Lambton Harbour

TINAKORI RD
THE TERRACE
LAMBTON
BOLTON
FEATHERSTON ST
CUSTOMHOUSE QUAY
JERVOIS QUAY
ORIENTAL PDE
HERD
HAWKER ST
CLIFTON TCE
URBAN MOTORWAY
SALAMANCA
QUAY
VICTORIA
MAJORIBANKS ST
CABLE ST
Te Papa
WAKEFIELD ST
BOULCOTT
WILLIS STREET
THE TERRACE
MANNERS
DIXON ST
COURTENAY PLACE
ELIZABETH
CAMBRIDGE TCE
KENT TCE
PIRIE
BROUGHAM

Northland
Wellington Botanic Garden
Cable Car

HARBOUR VIEW
WOBURN
NORTHLAND
CHISWICK
FARM
GARDEN RD
GLENMORE ST
NORTHLAND
GLENN
PUTNAM
RAROA CRES
CLAYTON
CHARTON
WAIAPU
MOANA RD
ST JAMES
NGAIO
GLEN
RIMU
UPLAND
GLASGOW
CENTRAL TCE
RAWHITI
UPLAND RD

GHUZNEE ST
TARANAKI ST
TORY ST
VIVIAN
CUBA

Kelburn
Shopping
Victoria University

PLUNKET
NORWAY
RAROA RD
HOLLOWAY RD
KELBURN PDE
ADAMS
DEVON
ABEL
VICTORIA ST
SMITH ST
ARTHUR
WEBB
BUCKLE ST
Te Aro

Aro Valley
Shopping
ARO STREET
DURHAM
MORTIMER
EPUNI
OHIRO RD
NAIRN
BROOKLYN RD
THOMPSON
HOPPER ST
TARANAKI ST
Massey University
Basin Reserve
ADELAIDE ROAD
KING
TASMAN ST

Karori Wildlife Sanctuary

George Denton Park
Highbury
HIGHBURY
KOROMIKO
PLEASANT
MT
LAURA AVE
KAREPA
BRUCE
TAYNERA
APUKA
Central Park
Brooklyn
BROOKLYN
BELL
WASHINGTON
Mt Cook
B/D NILL ST
ROLLESTON
WRIGHT ST
WALLACE ST
HUTCHISON
JOHN ST
HANSON STREET

ASHTON FITCHETT DR
KAREPA
MITCHELL ST
TODMAN
CLEVELAND
McKINLEY
TAFT
Penthouse Cinema
CONNAUGHT
MOFFITT
WHAUI
KRULL
KIMANA
DRANSFIELD
FINNIMORE
LIARDET ST
McCOLL
Mace Pa

Meridian Energy Wind Turbine

BUTT
MORNINGTON
MILLS ROAD
OHIRO RD
VIRGINIA
Mornington
THE RIDGEWAY
HAVELOCK
FARNHAM ST
BALFOUR
PRISCILLA
Map 9

North

Map 7

Point Halswell

Kau Bay

Massey Memorial

MASSEY ROAD

Scenic Drive

ROAD

BAY

Maupuia

Point Jerningham

Shelly Bay

EVANS BAY PDE

Oriental Bay

ORIENTAL PDE

THE CRESCENT

MAIDAVALE

Balaena Bay

SHELLY

Roseneath

Scenic Drive

Kio Bay

AKAROA DR

Band Rotunda & Arts Centre

GRAFTON

ROSENEATH

THANE

Oriental Bay

ROBIESON

MOELLER PALLISER

ARIKI

TE ANAU

KIO

KAKOURA

SHELLY BAY ROAD

AKAROA DR

HAWKER ST

DE

Mt Victoria Lookout

ALEXANDRA RD

UPOKO

MAREWA RD

RAKAU

ARAWA

HOHIRA

WAIPAPA RD

HATAITAI RD

KAINUI

RATA

Greta Point

MAJORIBANKS

Mt Victoria

RAKAU RD

HAPUA

Hataitai

MATAI

ELIZABETH ST

PIRIE

AUSTIN

Bus Tunnel

WAITOA RD

MAUPUIA

BROUGHAM

ELLICE ST

Town Belt

Mt. Victoria Traffic Tunnel

TAURIMA

Shopping

Hataitai Beach

Evans Bay

Map 6

Accident & Urgent Medical Centre

HAMILTON RD

MOXHAM AVE

OVERTOUN TCE

EVANS BAY PDE

Hataitai Park

RUAHINE STREET

Government House

ALEXANDRA RD

COBHAM

DRIVE

CALA

ADELAIDE

N

Wellington Hospital

MEIN ST

PICTON

SOMERSET

WILSON ST

COROM

HIROP

WELLINGTON RD

COBHAM DRIVE

TROY

TACY

CAIRNS

BRIDGE

TIRANG

LONSD

RIDDIFORD ST

HANSON

HALL

HENRY

KILBIRNIE

Map 9

CRAWFORD

Aquatic & Rec. Centre

CRES

KEMP ST

RONGOTAI RD

SALE

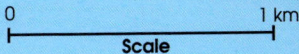

Map 8

0   1 km

Scale

Mahanga Bay

MASSEY RD

Scorching Bay

MAIN ROAD

NEVAY

FORTIFICATION

KARAKA

ROAD

Karaka Bays

BAY

RD

Karaka Bay

DARLINGTON RD

NAPIER

NEVAY

WEKA ST

TOTARA

North

MIRAMAR NORTH RD

CAMPERDOWN

REVANS

DARLINGTON RD

TOTARA RD

NEVAY

Scenic Drive

NEVAY

RD

PARK RD

TOTARA RD

AWA

Miramar

PURIRI

ROTHERHAM TCE

Worser Bay

REX STREET

AWA

BRUSSELS ST

TOWNSEND

MARINE

PDE

NEWPORT

SEATOUN

TAUHINU

BYRON

PARK

PARA ST

SEATOUN HEIGHTS RD

Churchill Park & Wahine Memorial

TAHI

Shopping

ATHENS

TOWNSEND

VENTNOR

FERRY ST

FALKIRK

MIRAMAR AVENUE

DUNDAS

MONRO

HECTOR

STONE ST

HOBART

CHELSEA

ARGENTINE

OTAKI

IRA ST

TIO TIO

Shopping

LUDLAM

BURNHAM ST

APARIMA

WILBERFORCE

BEACON

Seatoun

WEXFORD

ELLESMERE

DEVONSHIRE

IRA ST

TIO TIO

INGLUS

MANTELL

CALEDONIA

STRATHAVON

BROADWAY

CAVENDISH

HILL RD

BREAKER

CALABAR RD

KEDAH

HOBART RD

CRAWFORD

BROADWAY

MONRO

STRATHMORE

GLAMIS

THORNE

TANNADYCE

Breaker Bay

Map 10

Map 9

Map 6

Map 7

Kilbirnie

CONNAUGHT

HUTCHISON

HANSON STREET

HALL

RIDDIFORD STREET

WILSON ST

CONSTABLE

COROMANDEL

CRANFORD RD

KILBIRNIE CRES

KEMP ST

RONGOTAI

Shopping

Newtown

Carrara Park

DANIEL ST

OWEN

HIROP

ONEPU

BAY RD

QUEENS

COUTTS

ROSS

ENDEAVOUR

Shopping

MOFFITT

WHAUI

DRANSFIELD

FINNIMORE

LIARDET ST

McCOLL

STOKE

RINTOUL

ADELAIDE RD

RUSSELL TCE

DUNCAN

RODRIGO RD

BUCKINGHAM

Lyall Bay

MILLS ROAD

KRULL

KMANA

HAVELOCK

FARNHAM ST

BALFOUR ST

Macalister Park

Athletic Park

WARIPORI

Newtown Park

MANSFIELD

ROY

MANCHESTER ST

Wellington Zoo

Melrose

TAVISTOCK

QUEENS DRIVE

SUTHERLAND

FREYBERG

WHA

RUA

Vogeltown

LUXFORD

HERALD

THE RIDGEWAY

QUEBEC

PRISCILLA

BRITOMART

CHILKA

RINTOUL

LAVAUD

MT ALBERT RD

HORNSEY RD

Berhampore

DUPPA

Wakefield Park

HOUGHTON

MILLER

OHIRO ROAD

VANCOUVER

MONTREAL

HALIFAX

Berhampore Golf Course

DOVER

VOLGA

BUCKLEY RD

SOUTHGATE

BAY RD

HOUGHTON BAY RD

Kingston

DEE ST

JACKSON

TAMAR ST

RHINE

EDEN

AVON

MELBOURNE RD

VOLGA

HUDSON

Southgate

HAPPY VALLEY RD

MEDWAY

THE PARADE

CLYDE ST

TIBER

MELROSE

WITHAM

BUCKLEY

Haewai Wind Garden

TIGRIS

Island Bay

Shopping

MERSEY

ST

ALBERT

LIFFEY

MELBOURNE

ORCHY

RD

LANDFILL RD

MURCHISON

LACHLAN

JORDAN

RIBBLE

DERWENT

CLYDE

LIFFEY

THE ESPLANADE

HAPPY VALLEY RD

WYE

LIDDEL

MOSELLE

HUMBER

TRENT

REEF

Shorland Park

Island Bay

FROBISHER

SEVERN ST SOUTH

MILNE

OKU

THE PARADE

Owhiro Bay

HIGH ST

Taputeranga Island

OHIRO BAY PDE

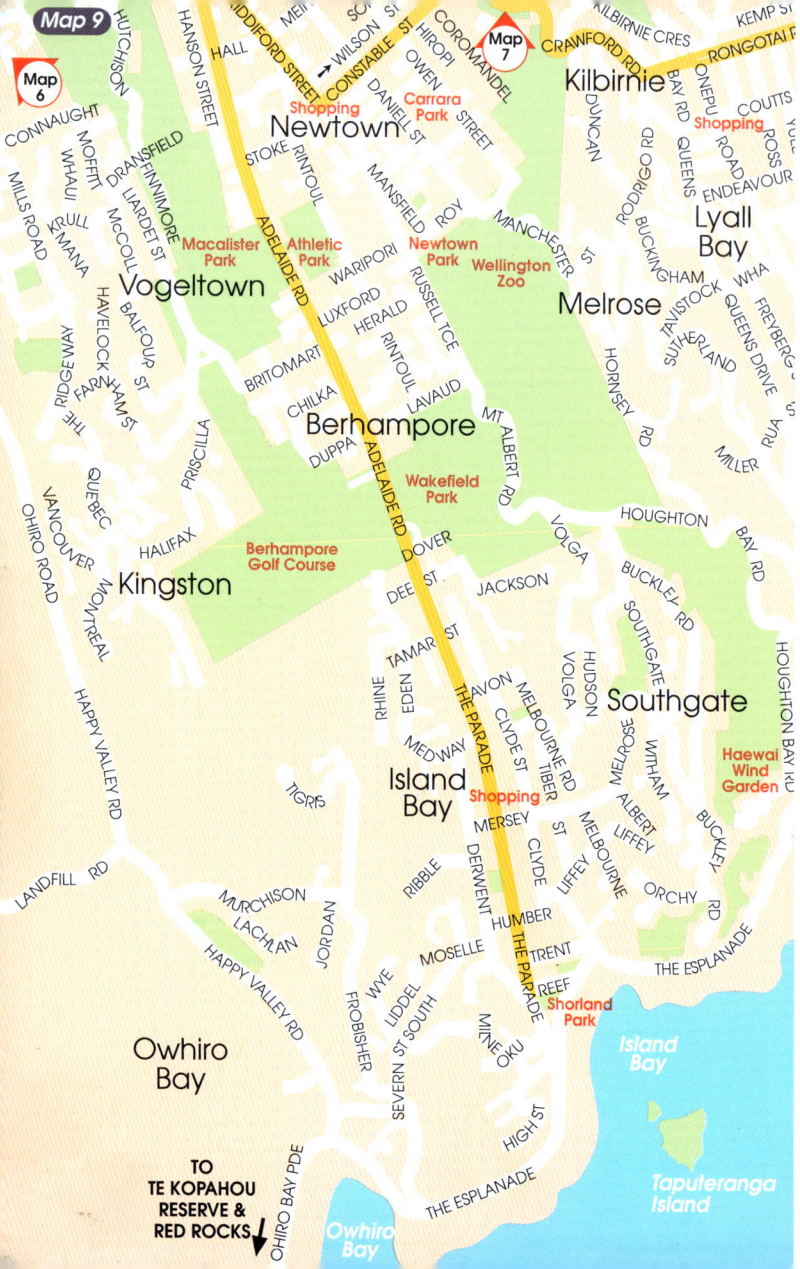

TO TE KOPAHOU RESERVE & RED ROCKS

THE ESPLANADE

Owhiro Bay

Map 10

Breaker Bay

KING

TANNAL

Map
8

LEVESON

MONORGAN RD

RATHMORE RD

AVE

BROADWAY

CRO

KEDAH

ART ST

KAURI

MIRO

RAUKAWA

Strathmore
Park

Miramar
Golf
Course

SIDLAW

BREAKER BAY ROAD

Scenic
Drive

BOWES

STEWART DUFF DR

COUTTS

Rongotai

BRIDGE ST

TIRANGI RD

LONSDALE

SALEK

ROAD

KINGSFORD SMITH

TIRANGI RD

GEORGE
BOLT

AHURIRI ST

KEPERENGA

Wellington
International
AIRPORT

Ataturk
Memorial

PURU
APU

CRES

LYALL

PARADE

MOA POINT ROAD

Lyall Bay

Moa Point

ONEPU RD

MOA POINT RD

Moa Point

Palmer
Head

QUEENS DR

VIEW RD

HUNGERFORD

Scenic
Drive

Houghton
Bay

QUEENS DR

THE ESPLANADE

Houghton &
Princess Bays

North

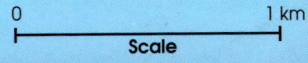

Map 11

CITY CENTRE

Scale
0   0.5 km

TO INTERISLANDER
FERRY TERMINAL AND
WESTPAC STADIUM

HOBSON ST
MURPHY
WATERLOO QUAY
THORNDON QUAY
MOTUROA

Thorndon
Pipitea

HAWKESTONE
MOLESWORTH ST
PIPITEA
MULGRAVE ST
AITKEN
Old
St Pauls
Archives
New Zealand

Wellington
Cathedral
National
Library
KATE SHEPPARD
PLACE
HILL ST

Port of Wellington
Container
Terminal

Railway Station &
Lambton Interchange

Parliament
Buildings
BOWEN ST
Gov't
Building
& DOC
Gallery
BUNNY

THE TERRACE
FEATHERSTON ST
WHITMORE
BALLANCE
STOUT

Glasgow
Wharf

WELLINGTON
URBAN MOTORWAY
STREET
BOLTON
AURORA
CLIFTON
TCE

CUSTOMHOUSE QUAY
WARING TAYLOR ST
JOHNSTON
Kirks
BRANDON
PANAMA
GREY
LAMBTON QUAY
HUNTER

Bluebridge
Waterloo
Wharf

Lynx
Queens Wharf

Ferry to Matiu/Somes Island and Days Bay
To South Island

SALAMANCA
CLERMONT
Cable Car
Kelburn
Park

THE TERRACE
BOULCOTT

WILLESTON
WILLIS
VICTORIA
HARRIS
MERCER
BOND

JERVOIS QUAY
Police
Civic Square
(See Map 1)

Queens Wharf Events Centre
Museum of City and Sea
Academy of Fine Arts

Lambton Harbour

Frank Kitts
Park

Chaffers
Marina
Overseas
Terminal

Oriental
Bay
Freyberg
Swimming
Pool

Taranaki St
Wharf
Te Papa
Circa
HERD ST
CABLE ST

ORIENTAL PDE
ROXBURGH
ORIENTAL
McFARLANE
HAWKER
EARLS

Kelburn

SALAMANCA RD
KELBURN PDE
GLASGOW
Victoria
University
M'way
Tunnel

WAITEATA
THE TERRACE
BULLER
WILLIS ST
VICTORIA ST
MACDON
DIXON STREET
DIXON STREET

WAKEFIELD
CUBA
MALL
MANNERS
MALL
GHUZNEE STREET
GARRETT
CUBA

Opera
House

WAKEFIELD STREET

COURTENAY PLACE
Westpac
St James
Paramount
HOLLAND
JACOBS
EBOR STREET
JESSIE
TENNYSON
LORNE
COLLEGE
TORY STREET

ALLEN
BLAIR
Downstage
MAJORIBANKS ST
Embassy
ALPHA

Bats

ELIZABETH ST
QUEEN
PIRIE ST
BROUGHAM ST

KENT TCE
CAMBRIDGE TCE
HANIA

Film
Archive
MARION
TARANAKI STREET

VIVIAN STREET
VIVIAN STREET

Te Aro

Tattoo
Museum
ABEL SMITH ST
MARTIN
SQ
FREDERICK
HAINING

ARTHUR ST
WEBB ST
BUCKLE STREET
National War
Memorial

ABLE SMITH ST

CENTRAL TCE
KELBURN PDE
FAIRLIE TCE
DEVON
ADAMS
Shopping
Aro Valley
EPUNI
ARO STREET
OHIRO RD
BROOKLYN RD
NAIRN ST
THOMPSON STREET
TORRENS ST
ARLINGTON ST
HOPPER ST
WEBB ST
TARANAKI STREET

SUSSEX ST
DUFFERIN
Basin
Reserve
Cricket
Museum
RUGBY
ADELAIDE
ELLICE
To
Airport
ALFRED
Accident and
Urgent Medical
Centre
TASMAN STREET
DOUGLAS
BROWN

Pipitea